DOLLAR BAY
MICHIGAN

COPYRIGHT
September 20, 2000

Clarence J. Monette
28218 Ninth Street
Lake Linden, Michigan 49945

All Rights Reserved

ISBN: 0-942363-53-1

Fifty-fourth of a local History Series

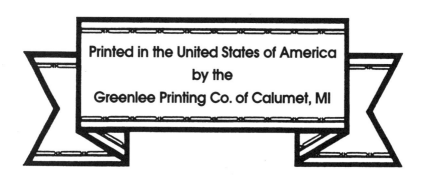

Printed in the United States of America
by the
Greenlee Printing Co. of Calumet, MI

AUTHOR'S NOTE

The data from which this book was complied were secured through numerous sources. From the many conflicting statements which appeared in the original manuscripts, newspapers and annual reports, this author has chosen the data and incidents which appealed to his reason, after all possible research, as being most accurate. If any errors are detected or important information missing, please contact me. These entries are a combination of many sources, most of which are listed at the end of this compilation.

Sincerely,

Clarence J. Monette
Author

DEDICATION

**Waldo R. and
Mildred A. Backman**

INDEX

This Houghton County community in Osceola Township is situated about four miles east of Hancock on M-26. History indicates that this village was named Dollar Bay because the bay looked round as a silver dollar, while some say it was named after Captain Robert Dollar of the famed Dollar Steamship Lines. However, Captain Dollar denied the honor of having given the place its title. He states it was named Dollar Bay long before he became interested in the area and lumbering in 1880. Several old timers say it was because the nearby Indians sold blueberries at a dollar a bushel. Dollar Bay's Centennial book states "That's where Ransom Shelden started his business which was called Dollar's Mill and under the management of Dave Dollar, so it became known as Dollar Bay." Take your pick.

History has it that the name Dollar Bay first appeared in public print in 1861. That year the Copper Country's all time top economic developer, Ransom Shelden announced in the Portage Lake Mining Gazette that he was going to build a sawmill on Portage Lake. He chose a site now known as the Green Spot, and a picnic and swimming recreational spot. His logs would come from what old timers called the Bollman Bush, which took in every-thing on the Keweenaw island surrounded by Torch Lake, the Lake Linden cuts, Portage Lake and the Gooseneck Swamp. Shelden's lumber would be shipped out in sailing vessels called lumber hookers. The men who worked the mill would live in boarding houses on the location.

Dollar Bay was a company town, and the area was settled as a lumber community when in the 1870's Captain Dollar built his sawmill there. After the timber in the district had been cut, the settlement was maintained by the Portage Lake Harbor. The nationality of people settling this town were Irish, French, Slovenian, German and Scandanavian.

This village is located on the north side of Portage Lake. When the village was platted, it was named "Village of Clark" after Joseph Clark who was the head of the Clark-Bigelow syndicate and the Tamarack and Osceola mines. Thus the village was recorded as such in the Houghton County Register of Deeds office. The post office authorities called it Dollar Bay because there was already a village of Clarksville in Marquette County. So now we have the post office of Dollar Bay serving the Village of Clark.

According to an article published in the Portage Lake Mining Gazette on October 6, 1887, the site of Dollar Bay (at that time) was owned by the Dollar Bay Land and Improvement Company and was situated in Osceola Township. It comprised of about two thousand acres of land, over nine hundred of which was heavily lumbered with hard wood. The greater part of this property was pine of which there were large quanities. These trees were cut to supply the saw mills of Mr. Shelden, who was largely interested in lumbering, and was once the owner of the land.

The ownership of the land changed hands several times. Years before, it was purchased by Ransom Shelden and Company for $1.25 per acre. After remaining in their hands for some time, it was sold to the Dollar Bay Mining Company for $25.00 per acre, who in turn sold it to the Osceola Consolidated Mining Company at $10.00 per acre. The Dollar Bay Land and Improvement Company, a company organized by the officials of the Tamarack and Osceola mines, had only owned the property since about 1885. (This was written in 1887)

The article goes on to say that this property was very valuable because of the water frontage which extended along the shores of the lake for about one and a half miles. There had already been erected a spacious dock adjacant to the channel at which the largest vessels were able to discharge their cargoes.

On the June 22, 1887, Articles of Assocation were filed with the county clerk by the Tamarack and Osceola Copper Manufacturing Company. The corporation was formed for the purpose of engaging in and carrying on the business of refining, smelting and manufacturing copper, copper ore and other ores, minerals or metals. Forty acres had been set apart for this company, on which they had already erected a warehouse on the dock.

During 1887 several dwelling houses had already been erected. A large boarding house built by Messrs.

Kimball and Thielmann for Mr. Warmington was constructed immediately adjoining the town site. Property at Dollar Bay, with the natural growth of the county, had advanced in value. Now with the Tamarack-Osceola people deciding to erect a smelting works there, property in the neighborhood was enhancing very rapidly, and lands in that vicinity would almost immediately double in value.

The town site, comprising of about one hundred and fifty acres, layed on a gentle slope and of which the highest part was probably some forty feet above the level of the lake. Its length paralled to the Hancock and Calumet railroad, which ran straight north 57 east and formed a convenient base line. It was about three thousand three hundred and sixty feet, and its width extending from a line about five hundred feet north of the railroad track, was in the vicinity of two thousand two hundred feet.

The main street connected the copper works and the through which the new county road ran, was sixty-six feet wide. There were also five streets, running at right angles to the railroad track, sixty feet wide and six hundred feet apart, and crossing these latter and running the entire length of the town lying parallel to the railroad track were seven streets, two hundred and twenty-four feet apart, these latter streets also had a width of sixty feet.

The blocks consisted of twenty-four lots; each fifty by one hundred and ten feet. These blocks

A post card published in 1909

were also separated in the rear by an alley fourteen feet wide. Those on the main street, however, were divided for convenience, so as to give a frontage of fifty-five feet with a depth of one hundred feet.

Mr. Maurice Swed remembered that everyone had big families and it was not unusual to have from six to ten children. Even though the houses were small, the residents usually had room for one or two boarders. The extra money was necessary to help out with family financing. He said that almost everyone had chickens and cows and that the cows were allowed to roam around town. Everyone had a fence around their property.

Avenue Granite was a dividing line with most of the householders being Austrian or Slovenian to the north and Scandinavians to the south of the street. On the west side of the town which was jokingly called the "400" or "Angel" town, most of the inhabitants lived in larger homes and had access to running water, as the water company did not extend their services to Swedetown. The population was a mixture of Norwegian, English, German, Austrian and one Italian family.

The Hancock and Calumet Railroad tracks ran through Dollar Bay, and it was expected that a station would be erected soon since traffic had already reached a considerable magnitude and the number of people using this rail-road was constantly increasing. According to a letter from Mrs. Charles

Pearce, the Mineral Range Railroad ran
an extension of the DDS&A and for some
time provided transportation and shipping. Later the Copper Range Railroad
extended their rails to Calumet with
two Chicago trains running daily, the
Chicago, Milwaukee and St. Paul. She
said that the Mineral Range Railroad
handled most of the shipping in and out
of the industrial plants. The railroad
tracks remained, although the railroad
companys changed several times.

     Dollar Bay was served by three
railroads. A February 1917 map shows
two sets of railroad tracks running
through Dollar Bay, alongside Highway
M-26. The Copper Range Railroads were
nearest the highway, with the Hancock
and Calumet Railroad tracks layed just
a few yards alongside. In 1885, the
Hancock and Calumet Railroad laid a
line at lake level from Hancock to Lake
Linden, thus opening an area for
industrial development fronting Portage
and Torch Lake. The Mineral Range
Railroads came in from the north,
running near the village, and served
the Point Mills region.

     The railroad era ended on Friday,
September 17, 1982, when a locomotive
and six cars of the Soo Line Railroad
moved to Dollar Bay and completed its
last commercial journey of bringing
railroad cars to the Portage Lake
District.

     The railroad had been operating
upon the request of area businessmen
trying to keep small businesses from
closing their doors. The extension was
granted by the Michigan Public Service

Commission but expired on September 30, 1982. Two of the last Soo Line Railroad cars to use the tracks were loaded with pulp from the Silver Forest Products and four others carried slag from the Peninsula Materials.

The 1887 article continues that quite an army of wood choppers, mainly Finlanders, with a few French-Canadians were engaged in chopping cord wood, which was sent to the Osceola Mine.

The soil at Dollar Bay consisted of a few feet of fine sand overlying two feet of hard pan, under which was found a deposit of remarkably clean gravel, which furnished at lake level a beautiful supply of good water over the entire property. The location was a very healthy one; the winters were of course cold, but the air was clear and very dry while the summers were delightfully cool.

Years before all of this development, just across the narrow entrance to Dollar Bay, and opposite the site of the new rolling mill, the the villages of the last survivers of the Keweenaw branch of the Ojibway Indians had stood. The remains of which were visable some thirty (1857) years ago, but frequent forest fires had obilerated every trace of their habitation.

In July of 1915, Father Miller of Dollar Bay addressed the Second annual dinner of the Copper Country Commercial Club. Part of his speech is as follows: "Mr. Price informed me to prime myself with a few remarks about the liveliest little town in copperdom.

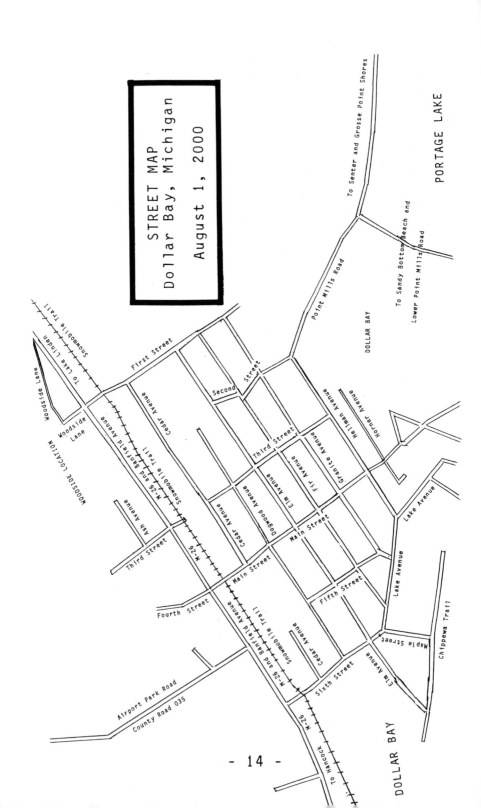

STREET MAP
Dollar Bay, Michigan
August 1, 2000

PORTAGE LAKE

To Senter and Grosse Point Shores

Point Mills Road

To Sandy Bottom Beach and
Lower Point Mills Road

DOLLAR BAY

Snowmobile Trail

To Lake Linden

Woodside Lane

Woodside Lane

WOODSIDE LOCATION

First Street

Second Street

Banfield Avenue

Cedar Avenue

Third Street

M-26 and Banfield Avenue

Snowmobile Trail

M-26

Ash Avenue

Third Street

Cedar Avenue

Dogwood Avenue

Elm Avenue

Third Street

Fir Avenue

Granite Avenue

Hellman Avenue

Horner Avenue

Main Street

Main Street

Lake Avenue

Lake Avenue

Lake Avenue

Fourth Street

Fifth Street

Maple Street

Chippewa Trail

Airport Park Road

County Road 035

M-26 and Banfield Avenue

Snowmobile Trail

M-26

Cedar Avenue

Sixth Street

Elm Avenue

To Hancock

DOLLAR BAY

And Gentlemen when I began to prime myself I felt as never before the utter paucity of the English langauage to do justice to the livest little town in copperdom."

"Dollar Bay is situated some where knee deep, along the great copper belt with Houghton county at one end and strike county at the other. Dollar Bay is like New York, London, and Shanghai, is in one important respect. There is only one of it. The man who invented Dollar Bay's name didn't patent it: but he was safe enough. No one has stolen it. For about 50 years Dollar Bay has struggled along and never has any ambitious city annoyed it by calling itself, "New Dollar Bay or Dollar Bayville or Dollar Bay Center."

"Thousands of people who don't know whether Dollar Bay is a breakfast food or a new kind of disease have lovingly murmured its name and have taken it home to try it on their pianolas. Everyone is familiar with Dollar Bay but few know whether it is an institution or is played like a piccolo. As a matter of fact Dollar Bay is one of Michigan's best known cities and is not otherwise peculiar. It began life about 50 years ago and in a short time had become large enough and strong enough to bear its present name."

"The population of Dollar Bay is not important as far as national statistics go, being about the same as Ripley during a championship game. Its monuments are its smoke stacks: mighty good things. Its streets are navigable by automobile provided you take those

Dollar Bay, Michigan - Courtesy of the Mac Frimodig collection

that are high: mighty bad things. The
Bays are not only prosperous and
enterprising but are happy and content.
This is because of the fact that when a
Dollar Bay man misses a train on any of
the city's railroads, he can always
walk the ties."

"Dollar Bay has become famous and
has been placed on the map for just two
things. In the first place we turn out
the best brand of red metal in the
world. An in the second place we
manufacture that best brand of red
metal into the finest brand of copper
wire to be found anywhere on the face
of God's green earth. When you come to
consider the size of this earth some of
you may say those are tremendous
assertions. Granted, but you will find
them corroborated by competent
authority down at Dollar Bay."

"We have no commercial club but I
want to tell you, that we are wide
awake, ready and willing at all times
to abduct any manufacturing industry
desiring to locate in this part of the
country. Whenever we have no
manufacturing industry worth abducting
we employ our leisure moments in
abducting one hundred thousand dollar
school houses. And by the way, this
$100,000 school of ours though but ten
days old, has a college yell as loud as
Harvard. Today you will find tourists
coming up to our far famed copper
region on the Copper Country Limited
passing through Chicago, Milwaukee,
Green Bay, Marinette, Iron Mountain,
Houghton, and Hancock without getting
out their magazines to breath, but as
the train keeps rolling along a little

further and the young man comes along
crying out "Dollar Bay next station,
Dollar Bay" they all begin to poke
their heads eagerly exclaiming: "Dear
Me, here's Dollar Bay. Let us see if
it looks like it." And as they stand
upon the platform and gaze upon the
little Emerald Gem nesting between the
green clad hills and throw up their
hands in wonder and admiration
explaining: "Well I'll be d--."

Citizens of Dollar Bay have always
participated in sports and Harry
Burbank establish a ball park in the
1950's. There had been two parks in
the 1940's, but both were in the
village and were eaten up by area
development. In the late 1950's, the
Dollar Bay veterans got involved and
began buying land where the ball field
is situated today.

In November of 1988, lots in the
village were purchased by the township
for more than $18,000. The Veterans of
Foreign Wars Post raised $8,000 for the
property it had previously purchased,
and Waldo Backman who had owned the
property, received $750.00. They both
donated their proceeds from the sale
back to the township. Bids were let on
the project in 1990, but even the low
bid of $88,000 was too high. Thus,
dugouts, restrooms and other parts of
the project were dropped.

Work on the field, including
raising it, providing drainage,
seeding, installing a backstop and
fencing the outfield, was finished in
1990. All was the result of
contributions of materials and labor,

right down to the portable privy
supplied by Jim's Septic Systems.

The current baseball field was
improved in 1992 and it was transformed
into an asset to be enjoyed by the
whole community. Some of the
civic-minded organizations to complete
this were the Dollar Bay Veterans of
Foreign Wars Post 6028, the Dollar Bay
Volunteer Fire Department and the
Osceola Township School's Parent-
teacher organization. The improved
field included constructing a new
three-hundred foot sidewalk between the
ballpark and downtown by the firemen
under the direction of Chief Bob
Mattfolk and a covered seventy-five
foot long barbeque pit which was built
by the PTO. Neil Marietta served as
the coordinator while David Joyal laid
the block.

The project was funded in part by
a Department of Natural Resources
recreation grant of $80,000, with the
DNR picking up seventy-five percent of
the cost and Osceola Township chipping
in twenty-five percent.

Dollar Bay has always had a
skating rink for their citizens. Many
rinks were privately owned, and were
usually located in the back yards.
However, Osceola Township and the
social welfare personnel now take care
of the public rink near the south end
on the corner of Main Street and
Hellman Avenue. This rink is usually
supervised. The township pays for the
water and lights and an attendant.
Free skating is usually provided from
seven to nine p.m. every day for both
youth and adults.

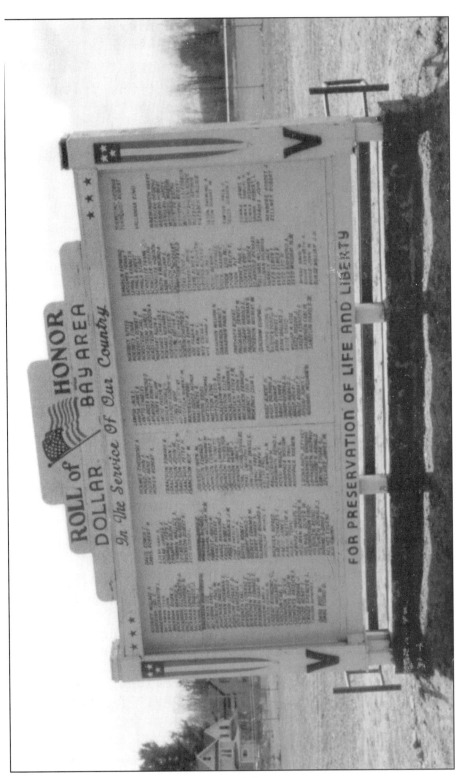

The Dollar Bay large white Honor Roll was first located on a corner of the high school lawn. It can now be found on the Main Street, near the baseball park, and is a memorial to those from Dollar Bay who served in the armed forces of the United States. According to the Daily Mining Gazette, Dollar Bay residents honored their war heroes during World War II when they raised more than $400.00 to erect an honor roll. One evening, a group of ladies playing pinochle came up with a plan to get other mothers together and do something to honor all the husbands and sons who were already in the service. By word of mouth, the information was passed around. During the winter of 1942 and early winter of 1943, a town meeting was held at the Dollar Bay High School. At that meeting the decision was made to build the honor roll.

The project was financed by soliciting door-to-door for cash donations. The ladies also raised money by organizing ice skating parties that were located where the Pioneer Park and fire hall are now. They sold hot dogs for ten cents and pop for a nickel. The hot dogs were cooked in water on top of a pot belly wood stove at the old fire hall according to Norbert Spellich. The women also collected scrap metals such as iron, tin and old household cooking grease which sold for 30 cents for a one pound can. Charles Engman, with his horse and wagon, collected the materials. Copper paid four cents a pound, iron one cent for five pounds, and old tires paid out five cents each.

The plaque was started in July, 1943, by Pete and "Bat" Blessant and was completed in June 1944. The Osceola Township School Board gave their permission to erect the plaque (honor roll) on school property. Mort Croze drove a truck and trailer donated by the Houghton County Road Commission to move it to the school. The total price for the honor roll, which was paid in full, came to $450.00. The honor roll was dedicated on Sunday afternoon, September 17, 1944, at 2 p.m.

The honor roll was moved to the baseball field when the school was remodeled. Much of the monument has been restored.

When the war ended, all the mothers and sisters who had donated unlimited time and energy joined the Bay Post 6028 Ladies Auxiliary when it became available. There is no longer an auxiliary.

From "way back", Sandy Bottom and the Green Spot Parks have always been popular from "way back." Sandy Bottom is now the Township Park and the Green Spot now sports private homes. In the old days this property was a camping ground for Indians from the Baraga region. They came there every summer to fish and pick berries which they dried for their winter food and also sold to the locals. Many of the old timers can remember having family picnics there, and the kids swam away the afternoon on warm summer days. Green Spot was the campgrounds for every kind of social bash, from Sunday School picnics to Fourth of July cook-outs. This author remembers going to Sandy Bottom when his father got home after work; the family would eat their evening meal under the oak trees.

During August of 1979, Osceola Township purchased this park, the old Sandy Bottom Beach, from the Copper Range Copper Company. The property across the road, once owned by the Copper Range Company, was sold to a private corporation who divided the area into ten acre lots for sale. The area was adjacent to the old Dollar Bay Sawmill site across the channel and the Foley Copper Products buildings to the front. The township improved the beach by cutting grass, filling in low areas, and installing fencing to isolate the parking area. Picnic tables and benches were also added.

Waldo R. Backman, Dollar Bay's local historian, has been very active in the village's businesses. He moved to Dollar Bay at the age of three, attended the Dollar Bay schools and is an active member of the First Lutheran Church. He also served as Osceola Township Supervisor during 1978, 1979 and 1981 through 1987. He served as a fireman and was a past fire chief retiring after 40 years of service. In 1947 Waldo and two other residents started a planing mill in this village. The mill was sold to the Coponen family in 1954 and in 1960 he purchased this company. He started a business manufacturing wooden shovels for the Atlas Powder Company. The shovels were used at nearby Senter and were also shipped to other plants of the Atlas Company. He worked at the Atlas Powder Company until it closed in 1961. Waldo

Sketch Showing
Subdivision of Sec. 33 in Twp N of R 33 W
And the Lake Superior Smelting Co Property
Scale 1"=400'   Feb 1-1912

DOLLAR BAY

ROEBLING

ROEBLING

ROEBLING

ROEBLING

PORTAGE LAKE

Saw Mill

Ice Rink

Dwelling 193

Co Dwellings

Dwellings

Wire Mills

Warehouse

Office

Dock

Smelters

Assay Office

Top Office

Blast Furnace

Dwellings

High School

N

- 24 -

Sketch Showing
Subdivision of Sec 33 in T55 N of R33 W
And the Lake Superior Smelting Co Property
Scale 1" = 400'   Feb 1-1917

- 25 -

25-T/2.6

had a retail store and went into building houses. In 1967, the company had 25 employees. Waldo was a Scoutmaster and later was the Advisor for Sea Scout Ship 236. He was awarded the Silver Beaver Award for outstanding services to boyhood by the Hiawathaland Scout Council.

Dollar Bay resident Clemeth L. "Clem" Banfield was a well-known businessman. He was born in Houghton on December 18, 1916 and died on November 1, 1999. At the age of 30, Clem opened the Dollar Bay Department Store which is now the Dollar Bay Linoleum and Tile Company. Clem was married to Elna I. Sved and was a member of the First Lutheran Church. He was community minded and was a member of the Church Council, Centennial Committee, Lions Club, Elks Club, C.C. Lodge 135 F.& A.M., Keweenaw Chamber of Commerce, Wyandotte Hills Golf Club, Copper Country Junior Hockey Association, Osceola Township School Board, Houghton County Multi-Recreation board, Scout- master, Houghton National Bank (MFC) board member, Salvation Army Advisory Board, Copper Country Association for Retarded Children, Barbara Kettle Gundlach Shelter, and a chairperson for Suomi College.

Headlines in the Daily Mining Gazette read: "Capt Dollar Dies", "Dollar Bay Named For Captain Robert Dollar", and Death Takes Capt. Dollar, Shipping Man - Upper Peninsula Lumbering Was Basis of Magnate's Widespread Fortune". According to our local newspaper, Capt. Robert Dollar, prominent shipping magnate and former

Upper Peninsula lumbering man, for whom
the town of Dollar Bay was named, died
yesterday morning (May 16, 1922) at his
home in San Rafael, California.
Another article in the same newspaper
on the same date, stated "News of the
death in California early yesterday of
Captain Robert Dollar recalls his
business interests here over half a
century ago. Dollar Bay was named for
Captain Dollar who established a saw
mill there in 1878. He subsequently
became a notable figure on the west
coast in lumber and steamship circles,
building up international trade and
establishing good will in China and the
Far East. He was reported to be the
largest ship owner in the world."
Another article stated that while still
in his adolescence, Dollar left his
home and eventually found his way into
the lumber business in Canada and the
Upper Michigan. Later, he came to
California and entered the lumber
business on a large scale. This led
him to shipping as he needed carriers
for his lumber. Mr. Dollar was ill for
two weeks and died of bronchial
pneumonia at his home. He was 89 years
old. His title "captain" was one of
courtesy.

One of Dollar Bay's better known
residents was James C. Dunstan. He was
a representative from the Second
District, Houghton County, from 1903 to
1904 and again from 1905 to 1906,
serving as a Republican. James was
born in Cornwall, England, in 1847 and
was educated in the common schools of
England and the State Normal College at
Ypsilanti, Michigan. Mr. Dunstan came
to Michigan in 1869 and settled in
Keweenaw County where he worked two

years in the copper mines. He then prepared himself for the work of teaching, which he did for fifteen years. In 1888, James worked in the lumber industry, real estate business, and then occupied a clerical position connected with the various copper manufacturing establishments at Dollar Bay.

Representative Russell "Rusty" Hellman who served as the represent- ative of the 110th district in the state House of Representatives. He lived in Dollar Bay all of his life with his wife Edith; they had three children. Rusty served nine terms as the Osceola Township supervisor and ninteen years in the House of Representatives. A Democrat, Rusty won about twenty elections against about fifty Democrats and Republican opponents. Mr. Hellman was very helpful in assisting many Houghton County people and organizations in obtaining grants and loans from Lansing. He is well remembered for obtaining used fire trucks for most of the Copper Country villages.

Rick Laplander was born to Finnish immigrant parents living on the southern shore of Lake Superior. He was one of a family of ten children and was fourteen years of age before his father pulled him out of school to help put food on the table. He found a job where his dad worked, at the Roebling Wire Mill. Over the years, Rick was promoted first to plant superintendent, and then to Essex plant manager. With the help of his relatives, Rick built his house on the foundation of a blown up nitroglycerine shed. This home was one of the neatest in construction and design. Ben Keplar of the Essex Circuit described Mr. Laplander "---a man of great knowledge and many experiences, a literal copper mill genius."

Dr. Carl E. Waisanen was not born in Dollar Bay but moved to the Copper Country in 1959. He was a professor in the Humanities Department at Michigan Technological University amd he later became the Academic Dean and a teacher at Suomi College. Married to the former Dora Koski, he was a member of the First Lutheran Church, Board of Directors of the Portage View Hospital, served on the Houghton County Libary Board, a member of the Lions Club and numerous other professional organizations. Mr. Waisanen received the Suomi Finn-Fest award, the Suomi College Award of Distinction, Educational Service Award and Distinguished Family Award. He was born on July 24, 1921, and died on November 20, 1988.

To avoid duplication several other very important pioneers have not been listed in this publication due to their story's being told in the Dollar Bay Centennial book published in 1987.

The Dollar Bay Literary Society was one of the community's first social organizations. This society was organized on December 27, 1887, with a membership of fifteen people; one year later, it increased to thirty members.

The members met on Wednesday evening, March 27, 1888 and elected officers for the second quarter of

1888. The following people were elected:

    President - Samuel Eddy
    Vice Predident - E. K. Hayes
    Secretary - Jennie Warmington
    Treasurer - William Staats
    Program committee - D. Davis,
        J. Dunstone and E. K. Hayes

According to Dollar Bay's Centennial Book, "A Temperance Society was organized in Dollar Bay in 1899. During the summer of 1903, a hall was built at 408 Elm Avenue, at the cost of $3,000. Originally called the Swedish Hall, it eventually became known as the Runeberg Hall. In August, 1903, sixteen people met in Dollar Bay to organize a temperance society. The first officers of Enighet Number 6, S.F.S.F. (Order of Runeberg) were: John Steve, president; Jonas Mattson, Vice-president; Matt Sved and William Hogdahl, recording secretaries; Matt Sved and Charles Engman, finance secretaries; and Victor Nyman treasurer." In later years, Victor went by the English spelling: "Newman."

"The Temperance Society "Nordstjanan" (The North Star) was organized in 1899 and a rival society, Templars of Temperance, was organized the following year, but the two societys united in 1902 under the name "Syskonringen."

"The Society members built a hall for meetings; and a brass band and a children's society was started." A wood-framed building locally known as the "Finn Hall and Temperance Societies can be found on Elm Avenue. The

This building was once known as the "Finn Hall and Temperance Society: The Finnish Apostolic Congregation also met here and is now owned by the Dollar Bay Linoleum and Tile Company.

May 20, 2000

Finnish Apostolic Congregation also met
here. It was owned by the Dollar Bay
Linoleum and Tile Company and is used
for storage. At this time it is owned
by Donald Treadeau

In August 1903, John Beck
organized the benefit society "Enighet"
(Unity) with sixteen charter members.
The first officers were president John
Steve (from Portom), vice president
Jonas Mattson (from Malax), recording
secretary Matt Sved (from Malax)
financial secretary Charles Engman
(from Korsholm), and treasurer Victor
Nyman (Newman) (from Pedersore). Both
societies were very active. They
cooperated in many festivities and kept
up high memberships. Upon merging in
1920, these societies became Lodge No.
8 Order of Runeberg with about 130
members.

Veterans of Foreign Wars Bay Post
number 6028, located on the corner of
Elm Avenue and Main Street, was
organized on March 25, 1945, with John
Joyal being the unit's first commander.
Their post headquarters first housed
the village fire department, when they
had only one vehicle. Part of the
building at this time was also used as
a change house for the village athletes
when they played in the park which was
located across the street. The building was owned by Frank Foley who sold
it to the V.F.W. for $120.00 after
World War II.

The Post's membership is very
community minded and have contributed
financially to many activities. They
donated annually to the 4th of July

The Runeberg Lodge Number 8 Hall
November 2, 1999

celebration, to the children's Christmas party and to the Little League Baseball. The Post also has provided property for the baseball field.

The first Post Commander was John Joyal who was elected in 1946. He was followed by Reynond Hiltunen, Willard Cadeau, Edward Johnson, Martin Wenberg, Raymond Sandelin, Toivo Dahl, Kenneth Anderson, Wallace Engman, Roy Isaacson, Samuel H. Sowka, Richard Norlin, Paul Dostaler, Wesley R. Carlson, Mervin Sastominen, Robert G. Partanen, Jan K. Strieter, Raymond E. Carlson, Robert Mattfolk, Patrick Foley, Robert Peterson, Kenneth Stevens, Arthur Wuebben, and Norbert M. Spelich. The present Commander is Richard Norlin who owns and operates Richie's Grocery in Dollar Bay.

An Auxiliary to the V.F.W. was formed on November 24, 1946. They were also active in community activities such as the Voice of Democracy, Santa's annual visit, a poster contest for elementary students, and the Arion Award, for a student with outstanding musical abilities. The Auxiliary also helped with the Cancer Drive, March of Dimes and United Way charities. The Ladies Auxilary is no longer functioning.

A youth organization called the Rangers for the boys and Rangerettes for the girls was formed back in September of 1929 by Eli Mattson. Its purpose was "to help boys arrive to manhood with a sense of strong personal identity and true respect for

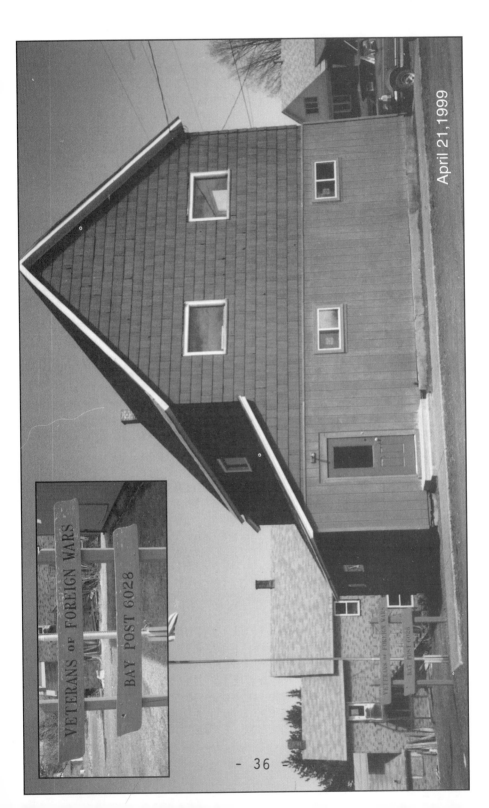

April 21, 1999

VETERANS OF FOREIGN WARS

BAY POST 6028

- 36 -

life in all its forms," according to the Dollar Bay centennial book. For nearly thirty years the Rangers and Rangerettes were one of the most active outdoor and sports clubs in the Copper Country. The Rangers engaged in highly competitive hockey, basketball and baseball teams. They also had outings, camping, hiking and motor trips outside the Copper Country and Michigan. They had two groups: the Senior Rangers and the junior group whose members were between eight and twelve. When first organized, boys kept joining until they had 35 members. The highest amount at one time was 86, but phased out to average 35 to 36 members.

The Pumpkin Center or Swedetown Shack is still remembered and should be listed under organizations since it served many local citizens. This landmark was located on the Point Mills Road and was a one-room cabin that was used as a watering hole by a group of local bachelors. It was written that a lot of beer was consumed in this structure. It was first built on the lake shore, behind the high school by the Waddi Gang who were competent carpenters. Bachelors who worked across the street at the Horner Flooring Company used to gather inside to play cards and drink beer. Whether inside or out, the cabin was nothing fancy. It consisted of one room, an enclosed porch and an attached wood shed. The cabin did not have any electricity and was heated by a wood-burning stove. When the weather was warm, the men sat outside in front and watched the bay. No one knows how the cabin got its name as the "Pumpkin

Center," but a group of bachelors in town purchased the cabin and moved it on September 10, 1947, from the shores of Portage Lake. In December of 1981, the Dollar Bay Volunteer Fire Department torched the old wood building. The surviving owners asked the fire department to destroy the building since it hadn't been used in several years and had now become a hang-out for neighborhood kids.

The Scouting organizations were quite active in Dollar Bay. The Boy Scouts of America, Troop 36, was chartered in February of 1925, under the sponsorship of a group of citizens. Meetings were held at the grade school and high school. Many years later the V.F.W. provided facilities for meetings. They then moved to the First Lutheran Church. Some of the Scoutmasters included C. F. Blethen, John Steimle, Thurston Helman, William Thomas, Walter Holmlund, Melvin Knott, Richard Hadrich, Raymond Franz, Waldo Backman, Paul Storves, Wilfred Milde, Wallace Engman, Bruce Kettenbeil, Jack Dugdale, Kerry Barna, Dave Clark and David Boutin. Scouts who earned their Eagle awards were Sven Backman, Waldo Backman, Frank Roy and Charles Sved.

Sea Scout Ship Number 240 was organized in 1956 with Waldo Backman as Skipper. They participated in many Council activities and several Scouts were inducted into the Order of the Arrow. This organization is no longer in existance.

Cub Scouts were active in the late 1940's and 1950's. Meetings were held

each week, with the exemption of two
months in the summer. There were
plenty of outdoor activities such as
cooking, picnics and hiking.

        The Osceola Township office build-
ing also has a long history. According
to local historian John Backman, this
building located on Lot 12, Block 29,
on the corner of Main Street and
Granite Avenue, in the Village of Clark
(which is Dollar Bay) was first
purchased by the Dollar Bay Land and
Improvement Company on July 12, 1887.
It then became the property of Johnson
Vivian Jr. and Company on August 16,
1888; Phillip J. Pearce on August 31,
1898; Thomas and Josephine Donlan on
March 23, 1917; Houghton and U.P.
Building and Loan Association on
November 8, 1928; Signe Dahl and Elena
Palosaari on December 19, 1939; Russell
Hellman and Leonard Christoferson on
July 7, 1948; Waldo and Mildred Backman
on November 20, 1968; John and Ramona
Backman on October 14, 1985 and finally
the Township of Osceola on May 28,
1997.

        Back in 1939, when Signe Dahl and
Elena Palosaari purchased the building,
the post office had been located in the
Schulte store building, but moved to
this building just before the Schulte
store was closed. Prior to moving to
the new building, Signe Dahl operated
her father's candy store across the
street located at 136 Granite Avenue.
When her building burned down, she set
up shop in the post office building and
moved into an apartment upstairs and

OSCEOLA TOWNSHIP

The Osceola Township Hall

April 25, 2000

took in boarders. Elena Palosaari who was working as a domestic helper, later became Signe's business partner.

An addition to the building was constructed by Carl and August Bykkonen. A variety store was put in the new part which sold dry goods, drugs such as aspirin, porcelain knick-knacks, sewing supplies, shoes, cloth-ing, pots and pans, soap, and Christmas toys. Elena would give instructions in crocheting. Signe and Elena sold the building on July 7, 1948.

Russell Hellman was operating a gas station across the street. When Signe and Elena offered to sell him the building, he and Leonard Christoferson bought it and converted the upstairs into two apartments and also put on a new asphalt roof. The post office remained downstairs with Anna Kindelan running the post office. The building was heated by a coal hot-air furnace.

When the post office moved to its new building in 1967, owner Waldo Backman completely renovated this rental space and added more apartments. Since Waldo owned the Bay Lumber and Supply Company, he was able to utilize the work crew and supplies of the company to cut out the floors and construct three floors out of the two-story building due to the high ceilings in the structure. There was ample room for a basement, three floors and an attic. Electric heat replaced the coal furnace.

The addition was rented out to Preston Glanville who set up a dental

Picture taken on November 2, 1999

lab. In 1975, Township Supervisor John Partanen rented the addition for office space to the township. A new outside stairway was constructed for the upstairs apartments. The four apartments were modern, comfortable, and always had a waiting list for tenants.

In May of 1997, John Backman sold the building to Osceola Township. Supervisor David C. Wiitanen said the first floor now houses the township supervisors, clerks and treasurers offices, a conference room, restrooms and one apartment, all which are handicap accessable. The second floor contains two apartments, while the third floor is only an attic.

Osceola Township was organized in 1886. The name comes from an Indian Chief who led the second war between the Seminole Indians and the United States.

On March 26, 1888, it was reported that the Town of Clark also known as Dollar Bay, was growing quite rapidly, and many new buildings were being erected. There was a fine two-room, two-story wooden school house, located centrally on Avenue "G", with an average of fifty children in attendance. This frame building was constructed by the Dollar Bay Improvment Company. According to the Centennial book, the two-room school was nearly completed in 1887 when it was discovered that the company had mistakenly placed it on a private lot. The owner of the lot was offered cash or any two of the company's many lots,

Picture taken on November 2, 1999

but no agreement was reached, and the structure had to be moved to a new site on Avenue "G". It was remodeled to a two-story building of eight rooms and deeded to the Public Schools of Osceola Township in 1892. A long covered hallway connected the school to the outhouse.

In March of 1888, Samuel Eddy was principal, while Miss Dunn was in charge of the primary department. Mr. Eddy and Miss Dunn were doing good work, and school director Haum, was congratulated for his selection of teachers. The building was painted during the summer of 1889 and some needed school supplies were added. Therefore the school was in better shape for the prosecution of another successful school year.

The Torch Lake Times reported on Tuesday, August 30, 1892, that "The school at Dollar Bay has been enlarged and improved during the vacation, and three teachers will be employed for the ensuing year instead of two. Miss May Uren will be principal at the school."

On the same lot as the wood-frame grade school, a brick grade school was built in 1906, which was also a two-story building. There were no high school facilities until 1915. After eight grade, students were either tutored independently or they worked with teachers under a course of study developed by the board of Education.

The present school began on Tuesday, April 7, 1914 when by a vote

of 103 to 3, the proposal to bond
Osceola Township for $75,000 . The
bond was to be used in the building of
a new high school in Dollar Bay and was
approved. The election was held in
Tamarack and a special train carried 95
Dollar Bay school electors to Tamarack
to vote at the election.

The election was a preliminary
step: merely the submission of the bond
question to the taxpayers and parents
of students. The township board then
arranged for the placing of the bonds,
size of the denominations and dates of
maturity. The township board also met
with the board of education, all of who
were in favor of the passage of the
bond.

Architect Hubert of Menominee
prepared plans for the new school some
time before. The drawings called for a
three-story, brick and stone structure
with the capacity for three hundred
students. The estimated total cost,
including equipment, was between
$85,000 and $90,000. The school was to
accommodate graduates of the schools at
Tamarack, Point Mills and other
locations between those schools and the
community of Dollar Bay.

The school would be located on a
site not far from the first school.
This site also afforded a place for a
spacious playground.

On Saturday, July 25, 1914, the
basement excavation for the Dollar Bay
school was started. The contract for
this construction had been given to Mr.
John J. Michaels. Mr. Michaels had
just purchased a concrete mixing plant

and did his own concrete work on the
foundation and the superstructure. At
that time he had nine skilled stone
cutters working on the cut stone
trimming for the building.

In 1938 both the brick and
wood-framed grade schools were closed,
and elementary students were moved into
the present high school. These two
buildings and the property were
purchased by Jack Foley in 1945. In
1949-1950 the Dollar Bay Fire
Department took over the property and
tore down the wood-frame building.
Some of the lumber from this building
was used in the construction of Rusty
Hellman's home. The brick grade school
was purchased by Jack Foley for $1.00
and was used to to house the fire
department until the fire hall was
built on main street in 1948. Later,
it was sold to the Dollar Bay Linoleum
and Tile Company which used this
structure as a warehouse. When the
company moved, they tore it down.

During 1980, it was discovered
that the Osceola Township School
District was in trouble; it had run
into financial problems. The voters
first bid for additional five mills was
defeated 310 to 196 in the June 9, 1980
election. The board believed it would
be forced to cut extra-curricular
activities or the students would have
to go elsewhere, according to School
Board President Dennis Barrette. The
district's second bid for a five-mill
operating levy was approved by 384 to
291 votes on Monday, August 11, 1980,
and the schools opened on schedule that
fall.

In August, 1993, the state fire
marshal closed a portion of the Dollar
Bay high school due to a long list of
violations. The school was unable to
use the basement of the building, which
included the gymnasium, locker rooms
and the industrial arts classroom.
Class continued, but many safety
provisions had to be made immediately.
Area residents had one year to decide
what to do with the building. Volun-
teers got to work in October of 1993;
the work was headed by a number of
individual contractors including Dan
Janke, Russ Dodge and Barry Collette.

The Dollar Bay - Tamarack City
Area Schools turned to the voters again
in 1996, and they approved a 7.83-mill
bond for the nearly $3 million project
which included a full size gym,
renovated four elementary classrooms, a
science lab, upgraded computer system,
and the expandion of its public
library. The elementary and high
schools were to be connected; thus,
putting kindergarten through grade
twelve students under one roof.

School expansion was finally under
way when the Daily Mining Gazette
reported on May 5, 1998 that the
Osceola Township School District was
finally breaking new ground. Yalmer
Mattila Contracting supervised the job
with a bid of $2.7 million.

On Monday, January 25, 1999, after
months of renovations and additions,
the kindergarten through sixth grades
were now housed in the Thomas R. Davis
Elementary School. All district

students, including about ten who received special education, were under one roof. Superintendent Dennis Barrette said that they now had their own special education teachers and class room. It was a resource room which covered a wide range of disabilities. The computers in the elementary school were tied into a network in which children shared access to many software programs. It was all part of the master plan to keep up in technology.

An open house was held on November 4, 1999, to celebrate the completion of the three million dollar construction and renovation project. It included a short program and was followed by student-guided tours of the facility.

Most of the information pertaining to the volunteer fire department was extracted from the Dollar Bay Centennial book. The department was organized in August, 1919. Prior to that time, fire protection was provided by the Lake Superior Smelting Company, but the smelter closed in 1919, and another method of fire protecton had to be found. Personnel on the original committee to organize a volunteer fire department were Silas Clements, John Schulte, Leslie Chapman, Frank Foley, Emil Storves and August Backman. Their first order of business was to raise $800.00 to pay for equipment, etc.

Their first equipment was a push cart which had two soda-adid fire extinguishers, each about five feet long. The second vehicle purchased

DOLLAR BAY
FIRE DEPARTMENT
SINCE 1919

April 21, 1999

around 1940 was a Reo type, which had been converted to a fire truck by Exley Horse and Carriage of Hancock. The Reo carried double forty-five gallon soda acid tanks. When it arrived at the fire, the tanks would be tipped so the acid would flow into the soda and water mixture, creating pressure and forcing the mixture out of the extinguisher.

In 1944, an old school bus was purchased and converted to a fire truck. At this time the only hydrants were on the west side of town, near the high school. The old bus/fire truck lacked good brakes, and in 1948 was replaced by a modern GMC truck. In 1974 the newest Ford truck was purchased.

The year of 2000 saw the department purchase a new freight liner, 2,000 gallon, pumper/tanker with all of the latest fire fighting technology.

The original fire hall is the present day V.F.W. Hall and was purchased from Frank Foley for $120.00. It was sold to the V.F.W. after World War II. The former brick school house was purchased from Jack Foley for $1.00 and was used to house the fire department until the fire hall was built on Main Street in 1948. The newest building constructed adjacent to it in 1968.

Fire chiefs have been Leslie Chapman, Vic Johnson, Bert Neveau, Arnold Sebbas, Waldo Backman, and currently Bob Mattfolk.

Frank Haun was Dollar Bay's first Postmaster being appointed on February 2, 1888. He started selling postal money orders on April 18, 1888. This pioneer merchant of the Town of Clark installed the post office in his general store, and he also carried a complete stock of all necessaries and Frank enjoyed the bulk of the town's people's trade when it was a new lumbering settlement.

The U.S. mail came by railroad. Mrs Charles Pearce (then a young girl) and her brothers transported the mail between the railroad station and the post office for three or four years.

Frank was followed by Antoine Schulte. He was commissioned on June 30, 1893. Then Frank Haun was appointed on January 13, 1898 and was followed by John C. Schulte on April 12, 1910, who was appointed by the President on January 1, 1917. Dollar Bay's fifth postmaster was Thomas J. Donlan who was appointed by the President and confirmed by the Senate on March 16, 1917. He died in 1919 while serving as postmaster. John C. Schulte returned to fill the position as postmaster on January 25, 1919.

Seven months later, on August 8, 1919, Ronald H. MacDonald was commissioned as Dollar Bay's new postmaster. He served in the Schulte building, later moving to the building which now houses the Osceola Township offices on Main Street.

Miss Anna G. Kindelan accepted the job as acting postmaster on June 16,

1933. She assumed charge on July 1, 1933 and was confirmed as postmaster of this fourth class postoffice on February 6, 1934. Kindelan was appointed by the President on July 1, 1937 serving until 1946.

Just before the Schulte store closed, the post office was moved to the Signe Dahl and Lena Palosaari building which now houses the Osceola Township office and several apartments. The post office continued to operate in this building until the construction of the present building and was opened in 1967.

Elmer O. Hoyer was nominated on January 31, 1946, confirmed on February 18, 1946, then re-confirmed and appointed by the President on February 19, 1946. He assumed charge on May 8, 1946. Gwendolyn Wiitanen served as his assistant for many years.

Francis D. Morin was appointed on January 1, 1993. Frank began working for the post office in 1959 as a clerk and letter carrier in the Houghton branch, and became a postmaster in 1972. Morin had 30 years of federal service when he retired in 1985.

Michael G. Kumpula succeeded Mr. Morin on September 28, 1985. Michael had been a postal clerk at Hancock since December 1979 and now assumed the responsibility for serving a population of about 1,800 people. During the interim the office had been operated by officer in charge James Niemela.

St. Francis D'Assisi Church and rectory, Dollar Bay, Michigan
Courtesy of the Mac Frimodig collection

Dollar Bay serves its residents through locked boxes located in the post office. It has neither city nor rural delivery routes. The current postoffice building is located on the corner of Fourth Street and Avenue Cedar and is owned by Helen Smith. It is a one story wood-frame structusre built in 1967 with a modern white and red sandstone front, with glass and aluminum doors. This building is used for postal services only.

The St. Francis d'Assis Church of Dollar Bay was one of the first churches to serve the community of Dollar Bay Being only four miles from Houghton or Hancock, the first Catholic residents attended religious services at either of the two places, often by trekking a path on the frozen lake. Frank Haun, the town's first merchant, first hosteler and first postmaster, brought about the founding of St. Francis' Parish. Frank was of Bavarian extraction and was Roman Catholic.

As the number of Catholics increased, mass was said for their benefit by one of the Hancock priests in the Dollar Bay school house. The initial collection for building a church was made by Father Hoeber.

Two lots, situated on Fir Avenue, were donated by the Dollar Bay Land and Improvement Company. During the summer of 1892, the church was completed and was blessed by Bishop John Vertin of the Marquette Diocese, on November 6, 1892. The Rev. Joseph Dupasquier was the first pastor, being installed on

October 30, 1892. A vacancy occurred
by December 14th of that year. Fathers
Atfield of St. Patrick's Hancock and
Father Joisten of St. Ignatius' of
Houghton took care of the parish until
Father A. J. Doser became pastor just
before Christmas.

Father Doser had the rectory built
and later departed on December 9, 1894.
Father H. Zimmerman came to the parish
on March 16, 1895 and left on December
10, 1899. In 1901, Father James Miller
arrived and found the parish without
debt. Due to an increase in the parish
membership, in 1901, the church was
lengthened by thirty feet, furnished
three altars, a confessional,
communion railing, statuary and
stations of the cross. A hot air
furnace was also installed all at a
cost of four thousand dollars. One
thousand dollars was also spent on the
rectory and the yard. At this time the
parish consisted of one hundred and ten
families. They were of French, Irish,
Slovenian, Austrian and German descent.

As an influx of residents
increased, a mission church was
established at Grosse Point about three
miles away. There were about forty
families, mostly French Canadian. Mass
was said there every other Sunday. A
quote from Father Miller's memories was
"When we got through building the
little church, I went to see James
MacNaughton, Superintendent for the
Calumet and Hecla Mining Company. I
told him that his fine men had built a
beautiful little chapel and that after
it was finished I got a bill of $200.00

for cement. Mr. MacNaughton wrote a note: 'Cement for Father Miller O.K.' and that was the end of the bill." This mission was closed in the early 1920s.

St. Francis became a mission church of the Hancock parish after the departure of Father Louis C. Cappo. A 75th anniversary was celebrated on July 23, 1967. Bishop Leo Blaïse, the Auxiliary Bishop of Montreal. He was born in Dollar Bay on April 27, 1904, and was baptized by Father James Miller. The celebrant of the mass was Bishop Blaise. A banquet was held at the Memorial Union on the Michigan Technological University campus in Houghton.

The First Lutheran Church of Dollar Bay is a congregation of the Evangelical Lutheran Church. It came into existence in 1900. Early residents of Dollar Bay met in the Finnish Temper- ance Hall and at the home of John Martin. J. Gust Nikander and John Back of Hancock, Finnish pastors, served the people in marriages, baptisms, confirmations, funerals and occasional services.

The first members of the church were immigrants who had come from the north, many from the Swedish speaking areas of Korsholm, Finland. The first services prior to 1900 were in the home of John Martin. Rev. J.T.O. Olander had a large congregation in Calumet and occasionally held services for the Dollar Bay Residents in the Finnish Hall.

On September 25, 1900, an

First Lutheran Church
(Entrance window reads "EV. LUTH. CHURCH")
as seen on November 2, 1999

- 58 -

organizational meeting was held in John Martin's home to form a congregation, but to erase doubts that official procedures were followed, a reorganizational meeting was held on March 12, 1902. Pastor J.T.O. Olander was in charge and Mr. August Boatman was appointed as the secretary.

A church located at 300 Avenue G, was built by men of the parish under the leadership of Matt Sved in 1902, the church known as the Finnish Swedish Evangelical Lutheran Church. By the end of 1903 the congregation had 141 members.

On May 26, 1930, it was changed to the present name. As years progressed, the members were served by pastors who also served parishes of Salem Lutheran in Hancock and Carmel Lutheran in Calumet. But after Salem Lutheran and St. Matthew Lutheran of Hancock merged to form Gloria Dei Lutheran in 1955 and Carmel Lutheran and Bethlehem Lutheran in Calumet merged to become Faith Lutheran in 1964, First Lutheran became an independanct church. Members did not choose to merge with either.

The name "Finnish Swedish Evangelical Lutheran Church" was changed to the "First Lutheran Church" on May 26, 1930.

From 1964 to July 1967, when the Rev. Gerald Erickson accepted the call as the first independent resident pastor, the Revs. John Simonson, a former pastor of the Church and Robert V. Langseth of Calumet served in the pulpit.

In 1946 the parsonage was moved to the Christoferson house in Dollar Bay and in 1949 a parsonage was purchased from the Copper Country Cheese Co-op for $4,000.00. The First Lutheran Church no longer has a parsonage.

In May of 1974, work began on the addition which would double the size of the church's facilities. This church's addition, costing $44,000.00 was dedicated on February 9, 1975. It provided Sunday School classrooms and a wide variety of facilities of church and community related endeavors.

Under the leadership of First Lutheran's pastor, Rev. Jay Schrimpf, the congregation broke ground on a $225,000 addition and renovation. The ground breaking ceremony took place on May 12, 1996. This project included the construction of an addition which served as a main entrance and housed a new elevator. Substantial changes were made to the sanctuary, renovation to the fellowship areas, and the construction of a handicapped accessible lavatory.

The contractors for the project included Anderson Construction Inc. of Chassell, The Metal Shop Inc. of Hancock, Bay Electrical Inc. of Dollar Bay; Dollar Bay Linoleum and Tile Inc., and Otis Elevator Inc. Traverse Engineering Services Inc. of Hancock provided the engineering services, with Dennis Lahikainen providing design concepts. During construction, the congregation worshipped at the Runeberg Lodge Hall.

Organizations that have served the church have been the Ladies Aid Society, the Women's Mission Society, the Ruth Circle, the Lutheran Brotherhood and a Luther League. Pastor Simonson served the parish the longest term, twenty-four years.

The Bethany Baptist Church is located on the corner of Main Street and Avenue "G". This is not the original church of the congregation which traces its history to a group of Swedish people who were brought together by the Rev. Axel Edwards in March 1922. During that year, services were held at the home of Mr. and Mrs. Matt Nordbeck and continued to be held in other homes.

A organizational meeting suggested by the Rev. Andrew Blomquist, an independent missionary, was held on July 16, 1923, at the home of Eric Johnson. Those present elected John Steve to lead all services. He served for ten years and also directed the Sunday School for the first three years. All services were conducted in Swedish, except for a monthly young peoples meeting for Swedish and Finnish youth.

The first church was obtained during the term of the Rev. Axel Edwards from 1924 to 1925. It was a former Episcopal Church, later the Church of God, and was the place of worship until the current church was purchased on July 18, 1944, which was a former Methodist Church.

At that time, the Rev. Martin Strolle was the pastor and also served

The Bethany Baptist Church - November 2, 1999

the Calvary/Baptist Church in Hancock.
On January 7, 1953, the congregations
decided to have their own pastors, the
Rev. Glen Williams accepting on January
25, 1953.

On March 14, 1965, during the
pastorship of the Rev. James Mitchell,
a dedication of a new addition was
held. It contained a modern nursery, a
ladies rest room and three classrooms.

During 1982, the Rev. Lawrence
Manzer served a congregation numbering
approximately 100. Parishioners were
from Dollar Bay, Houghton, Lake Linden
and Traprock. A mini-bus was purchsed
to serve the parishioneers.

The congregation celebrated their
sixth anniversary on Sunday, September
2, 1983. Dr. Joseph Stowell, the
oldest living pastor of the Bethany
Baptist Church, was present.

During August of 1986, the
congregation put up an addition which
served as the main auditorium while the
older section became a smaller meeting
room and child care room. The trusses
were put up on Thursday, August 28,
1986 with the help of a Julio
Construction crane and a number of
church members.

On Sunday, July 9, 1989, the
church members dedicated its new church
facility. The building now had a new
auditorium, foyer, modern restrooms,
new dining room, kitchen and Sunday
School classrooms. The new church
facility was designed, engineered, and
built by the congregation. It is
barrier free and will comfortably seat
185 people.

Jehovah's Witnesses
Kingdom Hall - March 25, 1999

Dollar Bay is the home of a
Jehovah's Witnesses Kingdom Hall.
Jehovah's Witnesses is a descriptive
name indicating that the members bear
witness to Jehovah, his Godship, and
his purposes. Jehovah is a personal
name that refers to the Almighty God
and creator of the universe.

The modern history of Jehovah's
Witnesses started in the early 1870s,
in Allegheny City, PA., now a part of
Pittsburg. In July 1879, the first
issue of the Watchtower appeared.
There are now more than 2,200,000
Witnesses in more than 200 lands around
the world.

The local kingdom hall in Dollar
Bay is the center for the "good news"
in the community. The area in the
congregation is mapped out in small
territories. These are assigned to
individual witnesses who endeavor to
visit and speak with people in each
home therein. The congregation has
elders to look after various duties.

Jehovah's Witnesses met in
downtown Laurium in the 1950s and had
their first Kingdom Hall which was a
converted warehouse. The Witnesses met
there until 1969 when the current
building was constructed and dedicated
in 1970 and was 26 by 52 feet. It
quickly became too small and a thirty
by fifty foot addition was put on in
1974 to meet their needs.

Members of the Peninsula Christian
Church held their first meeting in
their new log constructed church on

- 65 -

April 25, 1999

Easter Sunday, March 30, 1986. The
non-denominational, independent
congregation is dediated to the basics
of the Bible.

The church started with three
families which first met in the Hancock
home of Jack Carrel in 1982. Later,
they moved to the Houghton County Arena
and then to the Copper Crown Motel for
their meetings as their numbers grew.
During their development, an evangelist
of the Wisconsin Christian Missionary
Association ministered to their needs.

In August, 1984 the congregation
found a more permanent home when it
purchased eight acres of land on M-26.
Construction began in the spring of
1985. By this time the congregation
comprised some sixteen families. They
received financial help from Wisconsin
Christian Missionary Association, Lake
Superior Christian Church of Marquette
and numerous other churches and
individuals.

The 124 by 40-foot building has a
kitchen, expandable classrooms, office
space, a multipurpose room, and the
main sanctuary which accomodates about
200 people.

The congregation celebrated with
an open house and dedication service on
May 3, 1987, with an attendance of 119
people. As of January, 1990, the
congregation has been completely
self-supporting.

The Donlan House, one of Dollar
Bay's first hotels, was built in 1896
by Thomas J. Donlan. It was on the

Donlan House on Main Street in 1907. Courtesy of Mac Frimodig Collection.

corner of Main Street and Elm Avenue,
which is now the site of the Pioneer
Park. Later, this house was the
community's only hotel and was one of
the most popular hostelries in the
Copper Country. The building was 160
feet by 125 feet and had thirty
bedrooms, a large dining room, and a
lobby. The front portion was three
stories high and that in the rear was
two floors high. The last addition was
constructed during the war. The hotel
was closed in 1919 after Thomas Donlan,
the postmaster died.

It was purchased by W. S. Crebassa
of L'Anse and others according to an
announcement made on September 11,
1923. The sale was completed by Mrs.
Josephine Donlan, wife of the late
Thomas Donlan, who then returned to
Detroit after she personally handled
the negotiations. The strucure was cut
in two and moved to L'Anse on scows.
The building was rebuilt in L'Anse
before the winter set in.

The Cozy Theater building is
located on the corner of Main Street
and Fir Avenue, and was one of the
villages main sources of entertainment
when the town was a bustling industrial
center. People who played the piano
before the era of the "talkies"
included Rod MacDonald, Mrs. Maurice
Burbank and Mrs. Mary Gestel. Mrs.
Gestel also sold tickets in a glassed
in ticket booth.

After the theater closed, the next
owner operated a candy store in the
front of the building and a blind pig
in the rear. These two businesses were
separated by a wooden partition. The

This building was once the home of the Cozy Theater, then was a Blind Pig, then Banfield's Restaurant, later Kus IGA Grocery, Then Sackery's Grocery and now an apartment building.

April 25, 2000

blind pig sold moonshine by the glass, and the stock was hidden in a nearby garage. It was mainly patronized by the town's male population. A story has it that the place was raided by the "Federals" one day. When the police arrived, they told everyone to stay where they were, so the bartender sat down too. Anyhow, the police searched the room and could only find the bottle that the bartender had been using. When they left, the bartender got up and pulled another bottle from the case he was sitting on, which the raiders didn't find. The story goes on that the gentleman selling candy in the front section would have "one too many," and when the kids came in for candy, they would find him sleeping on the bench. Someone from the rear business would have to come up front to serve the customers.

After the blind pig closed, the building became Banfield's Restaurant and they specialized in making pasties.

The final business to use this structure was John Kus who operated a business known as The Kus IGA Grocery Store. He also sold a general line of groceries and is remembered as having a great meat department. His meat was never prepackaged. Butcher John Kolb cut or ground the meat while the customer waited. He gave the patron just what they asked for and needed. The building is now used as private housing.

The old building that once housed Jurmu's Grocery Store can still be found at 219 Granite Avenue. Matt

This was once the Banfield Store operated by Clem Banfield and Frank Starika.

February 21, 2000

Jurmu and Tom Matson were partners when
the store first opened. The store
building was set up a little unusual
for that time; when one entered the
establishment, the customer first saw a
drug store in a separate room on the
right then came the dry goods room
selling everything, include the shoes.
To the left was the grocery room which
sold canned goods, bakery, and such.
The middle room led to the loading
platform for truck delivery. In the
corner was the meat and cheese
department. Across the room from the
entrance was the office. Here the
billing took place, as most of the
customers charged their purchases until
payday. It also contained the cashiers
cage. The company used a trolley and
cup system to get the money and charge
slips from the various customer service
counters to the office. When one paid
their bills, the customer got a quart
of ice cream or candy, depending on the
amount of their bill. Matt Jurmu had
two teams of horses to deliver their
items to customers in Dollar Bay, Mason
and Tamarack. On one day a delivery
team would deliver and take orders on
one side of Dollar Bay and the other
side on the next day. Deliveries were
made in large tin baskets.

This was Matt Jurmu's second
store; his first was on Fir Street near
Banfield's current home. Here he sold
hardware and merchandise to farmers
which included equipment, seed and
feed. The railroad ran a track spur to
a siding on the side of his store due
to the large amounts of merchandise
ordered.

Only memories-pictures taken on May 4, 1984

Remembered too was Eli Mattson's Battery and Repair Shop, which he started in 1929. It was housed in a small wood-frame building with a large "Deep Rock Motor Oil" sign on the front and remains on the corner of Main Street and Garnet Avenue. Later, Russell "Rusty" Hellman took over the business. Rusty trusted and hired many of the village's young people to work for him.

Most Dollar Bay residents remember the large gas storage tanks located just off M-26. During May of 1945, the Dollar Bay Terminal Company erected three storage tanks on approximately 80 acres of land for the purposes of supplying the area with gasoline for a radius of one hundred miles. Products were brought to the terminal by lake tankers from a Chicago refinery. A new dock was erected and the fuel was pumped into the tanks through an eight-inch pipe line. J. F. Miller was the construction engineer in charge of the project and had built refineries in England and Japan as well as a number of plants in the United States. Each of the three tanks had a capacity of 840,000 gallons. All three were welded and steel constructed sixty feet in diameter and forty feet high. Each tank was individually surrounded by a dyke or fire wall that could hold the capacity of the tank and would keep the product from spreading in case of fire.

The tank farm later contained six tanks and was reduced to twenty-six acres. This was one of Amoco's smaller operations and had a capacity of 165,000 barrels of fuel, or 6.93

million gallons. It was stocked with
kerosene, a premier diesel fuel and
three grades of gasoline.
Thirty-seven years later, in May of
1984, the Dollar Bay Amoco Oil Company
officially closed the tank farm for
economic considerations. The number of
gallons that went through the terminal
didn't justify keeping it open. This
terminal served only seven dealers and
six jobbers, who would now be served
through Amoco's Escanaba terminal.
This was one of the three Amoco
terminals in the Upper Peninsula. The
company sold the 26-acre parcel, which
included the six tanks, to the Julio
Contracting Company of Ripley. An
Amoco tug-barge was sent to Dollar Bay
to drain the tanks before it was turned
over to Julios. The tanks were cut up
in October of 1994.

One of Dollar Bay's smaller
businesses was a Wooden Shovel Plant.
It started in August of 1959 and was a
factory which was not duplicated
anywhere else in Michigan. Owned by
Atlas employee Waldo Backman, the plant
owner did not hope to make a variety of
shoveling equipment. He was only
intrested in supplying the Atlas Powder
Company. Backman first located his
company in the former Finn Hall and
Temperance Society building, located on
Elm Avenue, and later moved to his
lumber yard on Hellman Avenue. While
at the Finn Hall, they only made wood
shovels; no metal trappings of any sort
were used. The spades were used for
moving dynamite powder or gelatin. The
gelatin is a material somewhat like the
trade dessert, Jello. There could be
no metallic parts because sparks could

be caused and would result in the
leveling of the plant as well as the
destroying of many lives. Backman got
the white birch for his shovels from
the woods near Point Mills. From a
good size piece of timber, some twelve
shovels could be made. Once the timber
was sawed and arrived at the factory,
Fred Rose began the job of digging out
the shovel blade recess, the handle and
the hand grip. After the crude shovel
had been fashioned, it was smoothed
out, sazd papered, and given a coat of
shellac. The center lumber strips were
used in the manufacture of pallets
which the Atlas firm used. The timber
was sawed in Svem Backman's mill. The
spades were shipped to the Atlas plant
by the Copper Range Railroad which had
a spur to the yards at Senter. The
spades were also shipped to many other
Atlas plants in other parts of the
country.

     Some residents also remember the
mitten factory which started in
September of 1946. The Foley Company,
with Jack Foley as the proprietor, was
making more than one hundred dozen
pairs of mittens a day and hoped to be
manufacturing other garments lined with
spun glass fiber, a new material
developed during the war that was said
to be several times warmer, more
waterproof and lighter than sheep and
fur lined clothing. The shell of the
mittens were of Aleutian cloth, also a
product of the war. The intermediate
lining of the mitten was a quilted
fiber glass which was extremely light
and warm The inner lining was a
plastic material made by the Du Pont
Company was absolutely waterproof,

pliable and durable. The fiber glass insulation was made by the Owens-Corning Glass Company. The factory was located in the old Dollar Bay grade school building, which with its more than 12,000 square feet of floor space, provided ample space. At that time the company operated a dozen machines and employed twenty persons.

Richie's Market is located at 112 Fourth Street in Dollar Bay and is the last remaining grocery store. The business is owned by Richard Norlin, a Dollar Bay native. Norlin opened the business, which was originally a schoolhouse located at Point Mills. Norlin said that his mother, Ina Norlin, attended school in the building, which was closed and moved to the Dollar Bay business district by her cousin Arvid Franz in the 1940's. The building also once housed a restaurant before it became a grocery store in 1958. Since that date, he has remodeled it and expanded its inventory which includes staple groceries, from lunch meats to dairy products, candy to pizzas, bakery, party items, newspapers, magazines beer, wine, liquor and lottery tickets. Norlin and his wife Theresa work in the store, along with part-time employees. Norlin does not live in the apartment over the store as he did before he had a family, but his home is just two blocks away. He and his wife Theresa have three sons.

The Portage Coal and Dock Company was originally named the "Union Coal Dock" and was first owned and built by

the Tamarack and Osceola Mining
Company. The dock and signs can still
be seen alongside M-26 and the canal
near Dollar Bay. At first they had two
big unloading rigs which were installed
on the dock and were steam operated.
The clam bucket was not in use here; a
large bucket container was lowered into
the ship's cargo hole, coal was hand
shoveled into the buckets and was then
hauled back out to be dumped on the
dock. The dock company had two hoists
with three men shoveling into each
bucket.

It served the interlake ships of
the Pickands Mather fleet of Cleveland
and locals watched coal being unloaded
from many steamers of the 420 foot
class which carried about 7,200 tons of
coal. For many years the larger ships
unloaded at both the Calumet and Hecla
Docks at Hubbell and at the Dollar Bay
dock facilities.

Coal was stored at this dock for
the Houghton County Electric Light
Company of Houghton. Their first
contract was signed on April 13, 1914.
During the 1924 - 1925, season 5,000
tons were stored there. Costs for the
power company were unloaded at 45 cents
per ton and storage and reloading on
rail cars at 22 1/2 cents per ton.
Other coal dealers also obtained their
coal here, and if they ran out during
the cold winters, were able to purchase
Pocahontas coal at $6.25 per ton. Coal
that remained during the summer due to
a "falling off of business" was charged
one cent per ton per month.

The electrical power company
complained because their coal was

The Portage Dock owned by the Upper Peninsula Power Company is no longer in use due to the John H. Warden Power Station in L'Anse switching from coal to gas.

stored in an out-of-the-way part of the yard could only be reached with considerable difficulty during the winter season, due to the large amount of snow which they had to remove. The dock company's dock and trestles were entirely of wood construction, and it was necessary to use a small swing boom hoist with clamshell to reclaim the coal in order for it to be moved from the coal yard to the electrical service station in Houghton. They felt that this was quite unsatisfactory and were charged 17 1/2 cents more for the unloading and storage than for coal handled by the Van Orden dock in Houghton.

Many Copper Country residents still remember passing the dock. After the coal was stacked for a long time, it would get hot and burst out in flame due to spontaneous combustion. Many of the coal piles were spotted with fire and produced black smoke.

The Upper Peninsula Power Company purchased the dock in 1972 from the Pickands Mather Coal Company who had purchased it thirty years before when they sold residence and commercial coal. UPPCO now rents out some of the property and uses the rest for their company maintenance and storage facility.

Partanen's Bar, also known as Dollar Bay's watering hole is located on the corner of Main Street and Elm Avenue. The bar is usually quiet but picks up by 6 p.m. when patrons sip brew with their neighbors. It was once

owned by Arnold Sebbas and later Dollar
Bay resident John Partanen. For the
past nine years Michael Busser of this
village, is the owner. It is the only
remaining bar in this community.

Herman Dahl's grocery store was
located at 130 Main Street, next to and
on the same side of the street as the
Osceola Township Office. He handled
the general line of groceries, with
bakery, fruit, vegetables, canned
goods, candy, and such. Many people
still remember him for serving the
biggest double-dip ice cream cone for a
nickel. Later, his sons Toivo and Roy
took over, running it for several
years. They then sold the business.

David L. Hebner purchased this
building and opened Hebner's Market in
1976, which was family run. Although
small, the store sold a complete line
and was amply stocked with meat,
produce, bakery, canned goods,
beverages, beer and wine. They had a
meat cutting department, which, some
residents insisted, featured the best
beef around. More times than not, the
market became the place where townsfolk
posted messages, such as notices of
houses for rent, garage sales and
community events such as bazaars or
bake sales.

In 1985, the store was sold to
William Latvala who operated it for a
few years. He followed the previous
owners with a general line of
groceries, and after a few years went
out of business. He is remembered by a
number of residents for his great deli

sandwiches. The building is now an apartment house.

The Dollar Bay Department Store was opened in 1946 by Clem Banfield and his brother-in-law Frank Starika. The store building was located on the corner of Main Street and Fir Avenue. It was the former Marshall Building. The building was a fire hazard and the State of Michigan required that the building be torn down. They rented the store, did some remodeling and worked on radios. Soon they put in a appliance line, floor covering, furniture, clothing and a shoe department. Later, Frank sold the business to Clem. In the mid-fifties, Clem dropped some of the merchandise and became a speciality store for floor covering. It then became the Dollar Bay Linoleum and Tile Company. A new modern store was built in 1974 on Highway M-26. The new building has 12,000 feet and is all under one roof. The old store on the corner of Granite Avenue and Main Street is now an apartment house.

Waldo Backman's Bay Lumber and Supply Company, which is situated on Hellman Avenue, was born in 1947 when he and Ted and Carl Sved began with a planing mill. In 1954, the company was sold to the Coponen family of Atlantic Mine. In 1961, Waldo Backman became the sole owner of the company, built up the retail store, and was soon also building houses. In 1967, the company had 25 empoyees. Besides homes, they constructed such buildings as the Superior Sausage Plant, the Davis Elementary School and the new post office. His son, John Backman, took over the business in 1983. The company sold all products in building construction, such as paint, hardware, roofing, siding and lumber. In June of 1987, the company changed from a retail store to a manufacture of commercial wood products.

Frank Haun moved to Dollar Bay and started a merchantile business. In 1888, A. M. Schulte became his business partner. The business went under the name of Haun and Schulte. In 1939, the now A. M. Schulte Company store, was bought to house the Copper Country Cheese Co-op and was rebuilt to be used as a cheese processing factory and creamery. In 1954 the Company moved to a new building.

The Sven Backman Saw Mill located on Granite Avenue, was built in 1963. It was first in Point Mills and moved to Dollar Bay. The logs being processed were owned by Northern Hardwoods, Ken Clouthier and Silver Forest Products. Sven operated a saw mill which cut a million and a half board feet in one year, and used crews from four to twelve employees. They cut fifty percent hardwood and fifty percent soft wood. In 1974 Sven installed one of the first modular mills which consisted of a head saw, log deck and edger, all arriving in Dollar Bay as one unit. This was one of the medium size mills. It was closed in 1997.

Dollar Bay's first public water system was installed in 1940. Few improvements were made after that.

Thirty-six years later, plans were made for a system to extend the water lines, make improvements, and to bring water to 329 more customers. It was on May 10, 1976, that a $220,000 federal low interest loan for this water project was announced.

It was in May of 1980 that petitions were circulated in Osceola Township in an effort to bring to a vote an estimated $382,000 water system improvement project. The dispute centered around the project's funding, which included up to $300,000 in revenue bonds at a maximum of seven percent interest. A question had also been raised about a hydrant rental fee paid out of the township's general fund.

The costs would affect only about 350 customers of the Osceola Township Water Supply System. The increase in hydrants would affect the entire township since the rental fee would come out of the general fund.

Township Supervisor Waldo Backman said the project was an "absolute necessity" being pushed by the State Health Department. Mr. Backman pointed out that an advertisement placed by the bonding company read "up to" $300,000; that the township also expected $125,000 from the Upper Great Lakes Regional Commission and had applied to the Department of Housing and Urban Development for an additional $120,000 which had received preliminary approval. The township also received a $5,000 loan from the Farmer's Home

An aerial view of Dollar Bay
taken on August 16, 1981

Administration. The township proposed a $1.00 per month water rate increase to help pay for the bonds. The township's water users were currently paying a flat fee of $5.00 per month.

The Osceola Township Water Supply System served Dollar Bay and part of a neighboring community. The rest of the township was tied into the Northern Michigan Water Company of Calumet.

The bond issue was approved and work began on April 20, 1981 by Yalmer Mattila Contracting of Houghton. The project included new mains on Avenues Cedar, Dogwood, Elm and Granite, located toward the east end of town. An addition was put on the pumphouse to facilitate a complete new electrical system, two new pumps, and a standby generator. An additional well was put into operation with the two pumps operating alternately. During the high water usage, the two pumps operated together. In case of power failure, a diesel generator provided power to run the pumps, which were operated by a radio control system between the reservoir and pumphouse. The construction of the pumphouse addition began on April 27, 1981, by the Locatelli Construction Company of Calumet and was completed by October 27, 1981. Coliform bacteria was detected in the water supply in December of 1995, so chlorination equipment was installed.

According to the Osceola Township 1999 Dollar Bay Annual Water Quality report, "Water for the Osceola Township water system comes from two wells located near Portage Lake southwest of the tennis court. The wells are screened in glacial drift and are screened to sixty feet deep. The wells produce about 350 gallons per minute each. Water is pumped to a 100,000 gallon ground level concrete reservoir located on the hill north of M-26. Water is delivered to customers through 4", 6" and 8" diameter water mains. Chlorine is added to the water to kill harmful bacteria. No other chemicals are added. The Osceola Township water supply is routinely monitored for potential contaminants. Reports of result of previous testing are on file at the township office and can be reviewed during regular office hours or by appointment." This report was submitted by Bob Mattfolk.

On the 22nd day of July, 1887, Articles of Association were filed with the Houghton County clerk by the Tamarack and Osceola Copper Manufacturing Company. The new corporation was formed for the purpose of engaging in and carrying on the business of refining, smelting, and manufacturing copper, copper ore and other ores, minerals or metals. The capital stock of the company was $1,500,000.00, and was divided into sixty thousand shares, with a par value of $25.00 each, of which $300,000.00 had already been paid in.

This new company had set apart forty acres on which they had erected a warehouse on the dock what was one hundred feet long by fifty feet wide.

They were also building a rolling mill building of stone, that was one hundred and ninety feet long by ninety feet wide, the walls of which would be seventeen feet high. The building would contain sheet and wire train and the necessary furnaces. It was known that this company would not have undertaken the erection of the rolling mill, unless they also controlled the smelting works. It was therefore possible that they would make terms with the Detroit and Lake Superior Copper Company for the acquisition of their buildings and plant at Hancock (Ripley), or would erect a smelting works at Dollar Bay.

The new copper smelter in Dollar Bay brought many smelter workers from the River Rouge district of Detroit, mostly of French, Austrian and Irish extraction, and all were Roman Catholics. With the building of the wire mill came a young man, Frank Foley, from Worchester, Massachusetts, to take charge of its operation. He brought several other Irish Catholics with him for the key jobs in the mills and to instruct others who came to work in the mills.

This smelter was quite modern for that day; the mills had revolving turn tables with molds. Workers brought the empty molds to the front of the furnace and men would dip out the liquid copper with long handled metal dipper and pour it into molds.

Township officials knew that the copper processing growth of this

View of Dollar Bay and Lake Superior Smelting Work's dock and copper on hand in 1916. Courtesy of the Lauri W. Leskinen collection.

business would increase the value of the property in the neighborhood and property in this vicinity would probably double in value.

The Hancock and Calumet Railroad built a spur track three thousand nine hundred feet long through the company's property. This track had two sidings, one of which would connect with the mill buildings and the other with the dock. Space had been provided adjoining the dock branch for storing large quanities of coal for the convenience of stamp mills and mines. Coal was off-loaded here and then brought to the mines in the empty rail cars after the copper ore was unloaded at Dollar Bay.

A large consignment of brick had already been unloaded from the ships, those being the largest vessels on the lake. The captains remarked that "This dock was one of the most conveniently arranged of any on the lakes."

The eight or nine hundred "piles" and the ten thousand to twelve thousand feet of twelve-inch flat timbers needed in the construction of the dock all came off the Dollar Bay property. The stone which was used in the construction of the rolling mill came from the quarry which was situated on the north shore of Portage Lake, from a mile to a mile and a half above Hancock. It was very hard and compact sandstone and was very well adapted for building purposes.

The site on which the rolling mill was situated was not up to the necessary standards at that time, and

Lake Superior Smelting Works,
Courtesy of Mac Frimodig Collection

the material for filling in, and also
for filling in behind the dock was
obtained from a portion of the Tamarack
and Osceola company's land, which was
considerably higher. By this grading
process, almost the entire extent of
about one hundred feet of marsh land
was filled up with the waste from the
rolling mill.

The railroad track, running to the
rolling mill, was situated at a
distance of two hundred and forty-eight
feet back from the main street, leaving
convenient business blocks of four
lots, which had a footage on two
streets and a facility of special
sidings for loading and unloading
goods. Since there was a lot of
railroad traffic, a station would soon
be built to serve the business places
and passengers.

By October 27, 1887, the company
had installed the iron roof for the
rolling mill. Work on the blacksmith
shop, carpenter shop and machine shop
was almost completed. The company had
also erected five dwelling houses and a
boarding house for their employees.

The following year, on March 26,
1888, Lake Linden's Torch Lake Times
wrote that they had visited the works
of the Tamarack-Osceola Manufacturing
Company and found everything in the
rolling and wire mills running like
clock work. On that Tuesday morning
they witnessed a circle being turned
out of the rolling mill. It was the
largest piece rolled since the mill
commenced operations, being 88 inches
in diameter and weighing 550 pounds.

Post Card - Loading copper at the Lake Superior Smelter at Dollar Bay, Michigan

It was shipped the same day to McMillan Brothers in Fayetteville, North Carolina.

In the wire mill, all kinds of wire were being manufactured, all orders for wire were filled promptly, and for quality and finish, the copper of this mill was equaled to the best. The manipulators of the copper in both mills were loud in their praise of the quality of the metal used. Foreman, Frank Foley, of the wire mill gave the Torch Lake Times editor a piece of copper wire that had stood a test of forty-four twists without breaking. None but Lake Superior copper could stand such a test.

Mill officers were increasing and perfecting the turning out of copper manufactures of every description. One of the furnaces at the smelting was ready for operation and would soon see the output of the Osceola, Tamarack and Kearsarge copper refined at this works. This would facilitate the economical working of the mills. On the docks one could also find copper being shipped by the barrel, each barrel holding 1,240 pounds of refined copper.

On Sunday, March 24, 1888, a fire broke out in the tin shop, a small building a few feet from the rolling mill, and the building was totally destroyed. It was unknown how the fire originated, but insurance would cover all losses.

The Portage Lake Mining Gazette reported on August 2, 1888, that the

Wire Mill, J.A. Roebling and Sons.
Courtesy of Mac Frimodig Collection

Tamarack Osceola Copper Manufacturing
Company had decided to erect another
copper wire mill on their property. It
would stand north of the present mill
and about thirty-five feet distant,
being built of brick for about four
feet up from the foundation. The
remainder of the building would be
constructed of wood. The floor would
be of either concrete or brick tile.
The ground dimensions were one hundred
by one hundred and twenty feet and the
height sixteen feet to the summit of
the roof.

The mill was divided into two
parts by a court. This allowed for
plenty of light, the northeastern side
being used for the drawing department,
while the southwestern side was used as
the annealing (cooling slowly to
strengthen and temper the copper)
department. This was said to be the
only copper wire mill west of New
Jersey, and that it would be patronized
by the western market, since there
would be a great savings in freight
rates.

The rod and sheet metal mill was
rushed with orders; there was a large
amount of work to be turned out and
shipped before the season of navigation
closed. Over 25,000 pounds of copper
bars were turned out on Monday, October
16, 1888. A fifteen lamp dynamo was
placed in the mill and was driven by
the twelve by twelve blower engine.

It was reported on October 18,
1888, that the rolling mill, machine
shop, saw mill carpenter shop and one
outside light was on one circuit, while

Cable Mill, J.A., Roebling and Sons.
Courtesy of Mac Frimodig Collection

the dock, warehouse, smelting works and wire mill was on a second circuit. The rolling mill was being run to full capacity.

The electrical equipment was a Thompson-Houston, purchased through Mr. Dee of Houghton. The new wire mill was powered by a compound Wheelock. Work would now be carried on at night as well as by day with the aid of electric lights. Any steam that was needed was supplied from the rolling mill boilers.

By December 13, 1888, the superintendent's house and offices were almost finished.

On Monday, July 14, 1890, the employees of the smelting works went on strike due to a difference between the works and the person in charge because of discharging men. Work resumed that Friday. The editor of the Torch Lake Times stated that "The successful mine management had not thus far proven a success in manipulating rolling mills and smelting works." The editor "regrets to see it retarded by incompetent management."

By 1902, the mining company's had expended much of their money on its mills and docks as well as the mine. Stockholders unacquainted with the actual conditions grumbled at the high charges for new work, but a big construction account was a healthy sign.

Horace J. Stevens wrote in "The Copper Handbook" for 1904, that the mills had seven stamps with an aggregate daily capacity of fully 2,500

Drawing copper wire at the Wire Mill on April 1, 1911.
Courtesy of A.K. Cox of Houghton, Michigan

tons of conglomerate rock. The heads
had been fitted with eight-inch
mortar-grates, opening into
quarter-inch mesh revolving screens
having Parnall-Krause hydraulic
discharges. Finisher jigs had been
replaced by Walfley tables. The
average cost of stamping a ton of rock
was 31.48 cents in 1900, 24.95 cents in
1901 and 23.30 cents in 1902. Water
for the mills was furnished by a
40,000,000-gallon pump. He also
reported that the wharves and steel
coal-sheds were the most extensive in
the Lake Superior district. A. Lincoln
Burgan was the mill superintendent.

Smelting was done at Dollar Bay
and Hancock (Ripley) in the works of
Lake Superior Smelting Company, which
was also in the hands of the Tamarack
Osceola and Isle Royale companies. All
mineral was taken from the mill to
furnaces in hopper-cars, thus saving
the cost of barreling.

The wharves and coal sheds of the
Tamarack and Osceola companies were at
Dollar Bay since 1895. They were
formerly at the mill sites on Torch
Lake, but the change of base saved the
ten cents toll per ton on fuel. This
toll was charged by the Calumet and
Hecla company (owner of the Torch Lake
canal) on all bituminous coal going to
Torch Lake wharves. The steel coal
sheds at Dollar Bay were among the
largest in the district and the wharves
were of great size, having been
extended in 1900.

A 1911 report stated that the
number one mill had five Allis heads,

three of which were compounded, and had a steel trestle approach. The number one boiler-house had four 200-horse power Pratt boilers that operated at a steam pressure of 150 pounds per square inch. The number two mill had two Allis-Chalmers steeple-compound stamps and was equipped with a traveling crane. The boiler-house at the number two mill had seven 200-h. p. boilers.

The joint pumphouse of the Tamarack and Osceola mines had two 40,000,000-gallon pumps and one 15,000,000-gallon pump. The two larger pumps, which were duplicates, had triple-expansion steam ends, with 22 inch, 40 inch and 60 cylinders of 52 inch stroke; the water end of each had three 30 inch plumgers and a 42 inch discharge pipe. The foundation for the newest large pump was 25 feet deep, in solid sandstone. The mills had a thirty by ninety foot machine shop, of sand-lime brick with a steel roof. There were a number of dwellings for the employees at the millsite.

It was proposed during January of 1911, by the management of the Calumet and Hecla Mining Company, to merge the Tamarack-Osceola in the new Calumet and Hecla Mining Company and to increase the capitalization of $10,000,000 shares of $25.00 par. This would give share-holders of the Tamarack twenty -two one-hundredth shares of new stock for each share of Tamarack-Osceola, and the owners of 47,386 shares, or upwards of seventy-five percent. This was formally voted in during a meeting held May of 1911. The management was now employing three hundred workers.

A reunion of several former Tamarack and Osceola Smelting Works employees took place on August 7, 1969, consisting of Eric Hellman, Emil Juntunen, Arthur Larch, John Stoor, John Spellich, and Carl Sved. Memories which were over 50 years old went back to when the company closed and there were some 16,000,000 pounds of copper left on the dock and in the warehouse. Carl Sved, who got the group together, told of when he unloaded copper ore as it came from the Isle Royale, Centennial and Tamarack and Osceola mines and when he unloaded coal from boats that docked at the Bay to discharge their cargos for the furnaces. Emil Juntunen remembered working for master mechanic George Kitto. Eric Hellman worked for the Tamarack and Osceola from 1905 to 1909, mostly working with the furnace. The men recalled that the Bay really was in the height of its industrial development when the smelter was operating. "Those were some of the best days of our lives even though we didn't know it at the time."

In 1912 the Tamarack-Osceola Copper Manufacturing Company was liquidated and assets were sold to John A. Roebling's Sons Company for $180,000. Although the company's works were in Dollar Bay, its main office was in the Houghton Post Office building.

By 1920 the Roebling Company claimed it had a yearly capacity of 50,000,000 pounds, but due to a lack of business, this capacity had never been reached. The mill employed seventy-

Emil Laplander, right, is pictured here in the 1940's in the drawing department of the Foley Copper Products Company. Courtesy of a Essex Group newsletter "Circuit."

five men, and wages ran from $3.00 for
a nine hour day for laborers to $6.00
per day for piece workers in the
drawing department. The consumption of
bars and wire in the United States was
fifty percent of the total production
of copper. The company was having
financial problems; interested people
were advised not to purchase this mill
until the local mining companies were
established and that there was a demand
for wire.

With youth and enthusiasm, John and
Francis Foley took over the old
Roebling plant with to make thousands
of miles of copper wire of all sizes.
Because of the considerable production
from the plant, it made for much
shipping. Both the Copper Range
Railroad and Mineral Range Railroad had
spurs to the property. Considerable
shipping by boat also took place.

In 1940, the Foley Copper Products
Company was formed by John Foley and
two officers of the Essex Wire
Corporation for the "manufacture and
marketing of copper rods and wire ...
to be turned into insulated wire and
cable." Rick Laplander was Essex's
plant manager.

The Dollar Bay wire mill provided
Essex an internal supply of copper rod
in quantities of roughly three million
pounds per month, enough to ensure the
continuation of operations in the event
of other copper supplier problems,
Oddly enough, much of the copper that
went into their product did not come
from the Copper Country at all, but
from as far away as the Pacific
northwest.

John Brzovich, Albert Neveau and Yalmaer Binoniemi in the 1940's worked in the Foley Copper Products Company wire mill to produce wire of a specified gage. Courtesy of a Essex Group newsletter "Circuit."

In 1945, Essex gained one hundred percent control of the company, they transferred the property to Diamond Wire and Cable Company of Illinois in 1950 and then to the Proof Company of Ohio in 1953. By the 1950s, many of the region's copper mines were closed. Copper mills in the area were importing copper from as far away as Chile, processing it, and then shipping it out to consuming plants, mostly in the Midwest and East.

The Dollar Bay rolling mill produced a copper bar of two hundred and twenty pounds, instead of the standard size of two hundred and fifu pounds qoduced elsewhere. The operation used about seventy percent more workers and more efficient operations.

The Foley and Essex Copper Products was closed on February 15, 1958, due to the distance from both raw materials and customers. Acting manager R. E. Laplander was informed by the parent firm in Marion, Indiana , that the wire mill would close by February 15, when all available copper would have been drawn into cable. Many of the workers had already moved to the parent works of the Paranite Wire and Cable Company in Marion, Indiana. The the 43 employees who were still working mill had decided not to move. Paranite was a subsidiary of the parent firm, Essex Wire Corporation of Fort Wayne, Indiana. Essex had also operated the Michigan Smelter at Cowle's Creek for a time.

When the plant was closed the rolling mill operation was

The 1889 nitrogycerin explosive at the Hancock Chemical Company.

disassembled. Part was sold and the remainder was shipped and installed into the Essex Wire plant in Marion, Indiana. During 1960 to 1962 the Great Lakes Boat Work manufactured mahogany Lapstroke boats. This venture only lasted several years. Herman Gundlach was the president while Jack Foley was involved. After this venture the buildings were vacant and never again felt the sweat of workers converting the region's copper into salable forms.

In the summer of 1963, Essex donated the property to Michigan Technological University Foundation Board, located at nearby Houghton, Michigan. That October, the Board opened bids on the property and sold the nine acres with one thousand feet of shoreline and fifty thousand square feet of space in ten buildings to the Julio Contracting Company of Ripley for $30,500.00. Julio purchased it to provide boat storage and other related uses.

One of Dollar Bay's earliest settlers, Mrs. Melissa M. (Marales) Schulte, wrote that officials of the Tamarack and Osceola mines organized a company under the name of the Hancock Chemical Company, erected a plant in their community, and began the manufacturing of powder for use at the mines. The company's officials filed its Articles of Association on November 1, 1887 and started to produce dynamite, chemicals, and blasting powder in January of 1887.

Officials built the chemical plant at Woodside Location within a mile north of Dollar Bay. This region was

known for its rock formations, which
were ideal for the packing houses,
mixing houses and finally the
nitroglycerin building. The company
hoped that if there was an explosion
that the rock would absorb most of the
shock. The plant wae also near a
Porgage Lake dock which was ideal for
shipping their product. Since this
location was still heavily wooded, wood
was used for the boilers. In 1895, the
Union Coal Company began to operate
their docks, and the company switched
their fuel to coal.

In 1889, a terrific nitroglycerin
explosion occurred in this plant,
resulting in complete destruction and
causing the death of seven employees.
It was the biggest of three buildings.
The remains of the victims were never
found. The plant was immediately
rebuilt.

In 1891, a forest fire threatened
the plant. As the magazine was filled
with dynamite at the time and it was
feared that the entire town would be
destroyed if the flames reached the
building. Since the men were all out
fighting the fire, the women and
children were ordered out of their
homes and were told to go to the lake
shore for safety. However, the flames
were stopped within ten feet of the
magazine and the town was saved.

This was largely due to John Sved
who worked at the plant. When the
building caught fire and everyone left,
he stayed and put wet gunny sacks
around the building, thus saving the
powder magazine. John was given a

reward by the company and with this money returned to Finland where he purchased a farm.

In March of 1895, the packing house was destroyed by an explosion in which six lives were lost. As in the first disaster, no traces were found of the bodies. Five of the six workers were boys. What caused these explosions was never learned. A local news paper reported that the loss to the company was estimated at $13,000.00.

In 1905, the Copper Range Railroad built a spur line to carry dynamite to Mason.

The Hancock Chemical Company was later sold to the DuPont de Nemours Company who closed the operations and had their employees dismantled the buildings. The Atlas Powder Company was erected at Senter in 1909.

Ransom Shelden set up a sawmill near the site of Greenspot around 1861. This early millsite was ideally suited to process timber for the growing mining and commercial industry as well as provide materials for residential construction needs. A lot of pine was cut and shipped out on lumber schooners and barges.

The saw mill belonging to the Dollar Bay Land and Improvement Company was destroyed by fire on Tuesday evening, May 19, 1903. It was the biggest fire on the Lakes for some time, resulting in a loss of about $50,000.00. The office and several other buildings were saved.

The first Dollar Bay Sawmill as seen in 1916. Courtesy of Ruth (Matt Folk) Willmes of Dollar Bay

The Tamarack Mining Company
started building their sawmill during
June of 1906. By June 20, 1906, the
first floor had been completed and work
was started on the upper story.
Contractor D. A. Eckmun had a force of
ten men engaged in constructing the
beds for the boilers and would be
finished in a few days. The three
125-horsepower boilers were from the T.
and O. Mills and were of the large
type. Each were installed on a stone
base, The boiler room was of steel
construction and was the only portion
remaining from the old mill. The roof
was entirely new. The smoke stack was
constructed by the McGrath's Boiler
Works at Ripley. The lumber for all
construction work was on the grounds
and the only cause for delay was the
weather.

The machinery came from a St.
Louis firm. W. J. Uren and Norman
Haire, officials of the Tamarack Mining
Company, inspected the progress on July
21, 1906 and were highly pleased with
the progress.

The Dollar Bay Lumber Company
filed their incorporation papers with
the Secretary of State in November of
1913. It was capitalized at $50,000.00
with 5,000 shares at $10.00 a share.
The entire stock had been subscribed
immediately. The incorporators were S.
W. Clements, Lifeu Hillyer, Mrs. Joseph
LaBrecque and Edward Clements, all of
Baraga. The first two owned 2,499
shares each and the latter two people
owned one share each.

The new Dollar Bay Lumber Company
leased the mill owned by the Dollar Bay

Dollar Bay Lumber Co.,
Courtesy of Mac Frimodig Collection

Land and Improvement Company for a
period of five years with an option for
five more if desired. Four camps were
in operation, three on the Mineral
Range Rail Road and one on the Copper
Range Railroad. These camps were
cutting 4,000,000 feet of timber, which
were hauled to Dollar Bay by rail.
Some timber logged at Huron Bay was
also shipped to the Dollar Bay plant.

The new Dollar Bay Lumber Company
had to just about rebuild the plant
which called for an expenditure of
several thousand dollars. They also
installed new boilers and a new band
circular saw.

A new industry started in Dollar
Bay During November, 1939. The Copper
Country Cheese Cooperative, made up of
four hundred progressive farmers,
banded together for the manufacture and
the distribution of American cheese and
pasteurized milk. The delivery of
pasturized milk began on Monday,
November 5, 1939.

The original articles of
incorporation, forming a non-profit
corporation were signed on November
25, 1938, by nine dairy farmers.

Their newly purchased building was
formerly the Schulte Brothers Store.
Modern equipment was installed in both
the cheese and pasteurized milk
departments after the building had been
remodeled to suit the needs of the
association.

Pasteurized milk was an important
item to everyone in the Copper Country.

All milk was locally secured and was subjected to a temperature of between 140 and 145 degrees for about thirty minutes to destroy bacteria. The milk emerged from the process sweet and wholesome.

Waino Kangas was one of the cheese makers, working here for thirty-five years. He had all of the talents and techniques in the production of Frankenmuth, Colby, and Cheddar cheese that brought awards and many blue ribbons year after year. His day began between four and five each morning as he got the plant set up for cheese production. He produced three tons of cheese each day. Most of the cheese was shipped to a major sales point, Kraft in Plymouth, Wisconsin.

In 1953, a new building was started and in March 1954, the Copper Country Dairy moved into the modern building in Dollar Bay. The new building and equipment permitted the dairy to produce a full line of dairy products. At the dairy, the milk from the farmers was pumped into one of the two large 3,000-gallon storage tanks, called the cheese tank and the bottling milk tank. The cheese tank milk went for cheese only, and the bottling tank for all other Copper Country Dairy products. Only Grade A milk could be used for drinking. This dairy had enough Grade A milk to be used exclusively for all products except for cheese, which was made from both grades.

The dairy was a jungle of
thousands of feet of stainless steel
pipes leading from one noisy machine to
the next. The milk pipes were
specially sealed to prevent
contamination and were periodically
flushed out with a cleaning solution.
The tile floors were wetted down with
water and occasionally a little stream
of milk and a vaguely cheese odor
filled the air. Milk was separated,
homogenized and pasteurized. The
gas-fired pasteurizer, which looked
something like a radiator, heated the
raw milk to at least 171 degrees for
sixteen and a half seconds. The
separator removed the cream from the
milk and added it back in the proper
percentage: 3.25 percent for whole
milk, 2 percent, 1 percent and skim
milk (less than .1 percent, usually
about .05 percent). The two percent
milk was the biggest seller, followed
by whole milk.

The most violent machine was the
homogenizer which kept the cream from
floating. At 2,500 pounds per square
inch, a set of pistons jammed the milk
through a small hole and broke up the
fat globules into a size that stayed
suspended. Cream that remained after
separation went into ice cream, which
had to have at least ten percent
butterfat, or butter. Cottage cheese
began with skim milk curds to which
cream was added.

By 1957, distributors were Wilbert
Juntunen in Marquette; Ernest Lamppa
for Ishpeming-Negaunee; Melvin Hill,
Harvey E. Kauppinen, Ted Wertanen and

Ronald Moilanen serving Baraga, L'Anse and Pelkie; Albert C. Jarvey at South Range and Painesdale; Frank J. Coon at Dodgeville and Chassell; Charles E. Heikkinen, Clayton Tuovila, Reuben Aho and Frank Coon at Houghton and Hancock; Carl E. Wuoti, Floyd A. Granroth at Hubbell and Lake Linden; Richard Aho, Carl E. Wuoti, Weikko Jarvi, Matt N. North and Floyd A. Granroth at Calumet and Laurium. Weikko Jarvi and Matt N. North distributed dairy products in Keweenaw County.

On Saturday, January 24, 1959, Urho Prusila of Toivola became the new president of the Dollar Bay Cheese Cooperative, taking over from Arthur Oinas who had been president for ten years. The association now had 500 farmers participating from Houghton, Baraga and Keweenaw Counties, and was doing a business of $2,000,000 per year. It employed eighty full time workers.

The Copper Country Dairy made headlines in 1977 when it was found that they were under severe financial stress, due, in part, to the alleged under-cutting of prices by three national dairies. At this time the dairy was a co-operative; one-hundred and ten farmer-members actually owned the dairy which they sold their milk to. This gave them direct conrol over their dairy products from cow to counter.

Under this system the farmers not only received compensation for the sale of their products to the dairy, but they also shared in any profits that the dairy made. This is where the problem arose. The dairy was no longer making any profit. Part of the reason was the surplus of milk which was glutting the market.

According to dairy spokesman Dave Larivee, three national dairies; Hawthorne-Melody, Fairmont Foods and Bordens were individually selling milk to stores at below-cost prices, undercutting Cupper Country Dairy. A law suit had been filed by Hancock attorney Andrew Wisti, but it would soon be too late.

Many of the farmers had $200,000 invested in their farms. The farmer and members of his family, often worked sixty to seventy hours per week. Governor William Milliken visited the dairy on Saturday, March 26, 1977, and he became aware of the current plight the Bay creamery was in. The dairy survived this problem.

Two years later, in November of 1979, the Dairy experienced a strike. Chris Kangas, secretary-treasurer for the Copper Country Dairy Employees Association said on Friday, November 2, 1979 that they were busy at the bargaining table. "We would like to get this settled as soon as possible. It's cold out on the picket line."

Management was offering an immediate 28 cents per hour increase and seven cents more after six months. The employees wanted 50 cents now, 25 cents more in six months and an additional 25 cents three months later.

This picture of the Copper Country Dairy was taken on May 4, 1984

They were negotiating a two-year
contract. That meant no raises in the
second year. The strike involved
seventeen workers.

The strike ended and workers
returned on Wednesday, November 14,
1979. The new contract provided for a
28-cents per hour increase and seven
cents additonal six months later. The
company also assumed a six cents per
hour charge for sick benefits.

By 1981, many small dairies had
fallen by the wayside. Even the
Bancroft Dairy of Marquette had gone
out of business in 1980, leaving the
Copper Country Dairy as the Upper
Peninsula's biggest. It was still
churning butter, cheddaring cheese, and
freezing ice cream. Milk no longer
left the dairy in bottles, but in paper
cartons, plastic bags or plastic jugs.

Dairy Manager Surjit Kamra said
that growth came slowly at a small
dairy. If the cooperative made a
profit twenty percent of the year's
profit went to the farmers and eighty
percent to the dairy. "With more milk,"
Kamra said, "we could find a market.
Membership in the cooperative was cheap
- only $10.00. Farmers were paid by
weight, with a standard based on a
butterfat content of 3.5 percent. If
the milk had more fat, the rate
increased. If the milk had less, it
decreased. The driver picked up
samples twice a month, and the dairy
tested it for the fat content.

Surjit Kamra, who was manager
since March of 1978, resigned on April

30, 1982. Harry C. McMorris was his replacement. The physical plant now handled milk from ninety dairy farmers and during 1981 handled sales that totaled $5,000,000.

On Saturday, September 21, 1985, the local newspaper front page read, "C. C. Dairy throws in the towel, closes". The co-op's board of directors meeting in emergency session, decided to give in to mounting financial pressues and closed the dairy according to board Chairman Leon Kallungi. The dairy had hung on in financial straits for nearly ten years. They had applied to the state for a $155,000 loan but did not receive it.

The dairy, which had twenty-seven employees and twenty-six member producers had applied for a loan through a Community Development Block Grant to Houghton County, but the grant was waylayed by objections from state departments that cited the dairy's lack of a license and failure to comply with environmental standards.

Dr. Jack EcEowen, head of the Emergency Management Assistance Team for Agri-Business of the Cooperative Extension Service and his team had been called in to manage the dairy in July of 1985. Fifty to sixty producers left the co-op because they were not being paid, which is why the dairy had lost its license and bonding in 1984. The dairy lacked permits for discharging wastewater into a lagoon behind its plant and for hauling its whey waste for application to agricultural fields. The disposal of whey ponds were

designed by the DNR ten years before
but were now no good. To do more work
was a costly issue and the dairy did
not have the money to do it. They had
also lost their license and bonding
from the Michigan Department of
Agriculture. The plant was now
outdated, one of the major problems
plaguing the dairy.

The Dairy Board was meeting to
decide how to liquidate its assets and
decided to begin shipping its members'
products to the Frigo Dairy in Carney,
Menominee County. More than $300,000
worth of local debts were deferred,
part of the dairy's more than $600,000
deficit. All employee wages were paid
in full by the time of the bankruptcy
proceedings, with the exception of
vacation pay. The Cooperative filed
for a Chapter 7 bankruptcy on September
30, 1985, at the Marquette Bankruptcy
Court. Actual business operations were
discontinued on Tuesday, September 24,
1985 since there was no hope for
successfully reorganizing the
cooperative.

Court appointed trustees tasks
were to inventory the equipment and
assets of the dairy and to establish a
value. A sale was then arranged and
the court decided how the proceeds
would be divided among the dairy's
creditors.

The Horner Flooring Company was
founded in 1891, by William Horner in
downstate Reed City. They moved to
Battle Creek a few years later and then

settled in the Upper Peninsula at Newberry in 1914. In 1931, the company moved to Dollar Bay and is still the main employer.

The unusual number of fires at the company's earlier operations had a lot to do with the move to Dollar Bay. There was a real problem with fires and the company decided to get closer to the raw materials. The raw materials consisted of northern hard maple, something that has always been in good supply in the Keweenaw Peninsula.

The first flooring mill building was erected by Samuel Horner who later turned operations over to his son Jack Horner. Emil Borsum of Newberry assisted in the setting up of the plant and served many years as a valued foreman.

Horner employees went on strike from November 17 through November 26, 1952. The firm's employees were with the International Woodworkers Union CIO. Under the new contract, the minimum wage was $1.05 per hour; the five cents per hour raise took effect on December 14, 1952.

In 1960, the Hamar family purchased Horner Flooring from Dave Horner and continued to manufacture hard maple flooring. Mr. H. Kenneth Hamar was president.

The vast maple forest of the Upper Peninsula and northern Wisconsin supplied millions of feet of lumber per year to the Horner mill which whittled it down into a variety of floor products. In the company's early days, its floors were found mainly in homes. The maple market later moved into the recreational sector, and Horner met the demand with both permanent hardwood strip flooring and sectioned portable floors designed for multi-use arenas.

In 1987, a portable sixty feet by one hundred and twelve foot regulation-size basketball floor cost about $47,000.00 and could be installed by a half-dozen people in less than two hours.

A Horner floor starts out as rough-cut lumber delivered from the sawmills to the company's plant, where the wood is dried in large kilns for up to two weeks at temperatures reaching one hundred and eighty degrees. Then the boards, which measure just less than an inch in thickness, are trimmed of knots and defects, finished with polyurethane and fashioned into two hundred and ten separate panels that fit together into one basketball court.

An announcement on August 12, 1988, stated that "Horner Flooring Company of Dollar Bay is the latest acquisition of the Houghton-based Ventures Group, Inc." Ventures subsidiary, Portage Holdings, Inc., purchased all of the Horner's common stock. Ventures was a "for profit" part of Michigan Technological University of Houghton, with Jon D. Marson as President of Ventures.

John C. Hamar was president of Horner Flooring at this time, being President since 1975. He had started

An early post card of Dollar Bay

with the company in 1959 and since that time had seen it expand into international markets. John retired in January of 1990, and his son Douglas J. Hamar now served as Vice President/ Chief Operating Officer. He had graduated from Michigan Technological University. Ventures Board Chairman Edward J. Koepel announced that Clark L. Pellegrini, Ventures Group President, expanded his duties to include President and Chief Executive Officer of the Dollar Bay firm; Mark S. Young would continue as Vice President for manufacturing. At this time the company was employing seventy-five workers.

In 1991, the company celebrated their 100th anniversary and were known for portable floors with no loose parts such as pins, bolts; cables or screws to hold it together. The "Pro King" floor took roughly one month to manufacture and was an outgrowth of an original model created by Horner called the "Sports King." A regulation basketball floor was made of 203 four-by-eight and 14 four-by-four foot northern hard maple panels which were assembled with patented hardware. It could be laid over other surfaces in less than two hours with a five-man crew.

On Tuesday, June 9, 1992, Horner Flooring Mill officials announced that "Citing a lack of materials and increased competition, Horner Flooring officials laid off eleven employees that Monday afternoon."

Tech Ventures started having internal and finance problems. A group of employees had submitted a letter to the media earlier that year, noting that problems at the mill were being caused by Ventures. Douglas Hamar said that negative press received by Ventures in some of its other holdings "hasn't helped us."

Horner Chief Operating Officer Douglas Hamar did acknowledge that Horner's association with financially-troubled Tech Ventures Group "hasn't helped" Horner and that the competition had used this against the company in the marketplace. It was obvious that Ventures, which could not even pay its delinquent property taxes to the tune of more than $640,000, was in no shape to help Horner. Suppliers knew of Ventures' troubles and demanded money for materials up front, rather than relying on Horner's good reputation as it had in the past.

A total of 72 people were employed at the Dollar Bay headquarters, 63 of those in the mill. Hourly employees at the plant were represented by the International Woodworkers Union, and the local president said layoffs had "been coming for a long time. He also said "I think it's a case of Ventures not having the money to buy materials." "I'm not referring to Horner ... they've always been successful." Employees in a written statement explained "When Ventures bought Horner, there were ample raw materials and ample inventory. Now we have almost nothing."

The Daily Mining Gazette announced on June 13, 1992, that "Ventures has agreed to negotiate a possible sale of the company to the Hamar Group." The Hamar Group was made up of former Horner Flooring CEO John Hamar, his Son, Doug, and son-in-law Mark Young. John Hamar, who had worked at the company for 32 years before retiring, said that negotations with Ventures would take place soon."

The employees group believed that the MTU Board of Control had the power to help keep the mill open and keep their jobs. "MTU could liquidate Ventures," one employee said. State Representative Stephen Dresch agreed and stated that "The MTU board is the responsible party. MTU would have to assume responsibility for Venture's debts if the corporation was liquidated." A university spokesperson said that $150,000 in unrestricted funds were transferred to Michigan Tech Ventures as seed money in 1980 by the Michigan Tech Fund Board of Trustees.

Sixty-three employees were laid off on Monday, August 3, 1992, for a minimum of two weeks. Horner employees felt that negotiation were being dragged out intentionally. Employees were back to work on Tuesday, August 18, 1992, working four days a week. Political pressure was exerted by State Senator Don Koivisto and State Representative Stephen Dresch. "We can't force them (Ventures) to sell Horner Flooring, but we can strongly suggest to the (Michigan Tech) Board of Control that some action be taken,"

Koivisto said. Ventures, a for-profit corporation, was operated by the university's not-for profit Educational Support Institute.

Educational Support Institute's board of trustees unamimously voted to authorize the Ventures Group to go ahead with the sale of Horner Flooring to the Hamar family. It would take at least thirty days while legal documents were prepared. Start-up operations began on Tuesday, October 6, 1992. The company was back in the Hamar family.

The Company is still growing, and the company's flooring is shipped all over the country; the business competes for local projects as well. With so many area schools constructing new buildings, business has been good. "Portable courts are our glamour product, but we produce many more permanent floors," said Douglas Hamar. Bill Gappy, who is Michigan Tech's winningest coach, came to the company in 1984. His many connections in the basketball world have been a big asset. Bill made a big impact with the company since he knows just about everyone in the world of basketball. That's a big help, according to Douglas Hamar. The company provided the court for the 1984 Olympic Games in Los Angeles and had done the same at the Pan American Games, Goodwill Games and World Games. It produces the floors the Detroit Pistons, Denver Nuggets, Toronto Raptors, Milwaukee Bucks and Utah Jazz play on, as well as Kansas, St. John's, Penn State, Detroit, Eastern Michigan, Temple, Wisconsin and Louisville. The

Horner Flooring Company is Dollar Bay's chief employer.

In 1990, the United States Coast Guard moved from its original headquarters at the North Entry to the waterfront in Hancock, a temporary site for a two-year stay. This Station performs search and rescue missions, maintains aids to navigation, and enforces laws and treaties on Lake Superior. The Coast Guard moved from the North Entry site for a number of reasons, including asbestos contamination and lack of space.

Finally on June 4, 1996 Station Portage conducted a ground breaking ceremony at Dollar Bay for its new facility. On Friday, September 5, 1997, representatives from across the Copper Country, Lansing, and Washington came to Dollar Bay to welcome the U.S. Coast Guard to its new home. Station Commander Chief Brian Williams said that in less than a month his crew moved all of its equipment and operations from Hancock to their new home in Dollar Bay. At the same time, they continued to serve the public by responding to calls for assistance and patrolling the waterways. Guardsmen were stationed throughout the facility to show those in attendance the many features of the new station.

This station, with a price tag of about $3.8 million, was finished a month ahead of schedule and within budget. Features include sleeping quarters for watchstanders and crew, a communications center, a galley, a

Below: The Portage Coast Guard Station as seen on November 2, 1999

United States Coast Guard
U.S. Department of Transportation

classroom and various maintenance
shops. The station, which has been in
operation since 1874, has a crew of
ninteen men, seven of whom live at the
station.

A 2,600-square-foot boat bay
allows Station Portage to store its own
boats in the winter. They can also
pull the boat in and do maintenance
work. This was not possible at the
temporary Hancock facilities. The
facility was designed by Hitch Inc. of
Houghton, and was approved by Coast
Guard Facilities Design and Construction Center Atlantic Division. MJO
Contracting Inc. of Hancock handled the
electrical and mechanical systems of
the facility and supervised contruction
by numerous local contractors.

This station on the Keweenaw
Waterway leading to Lake Superior is
expected to grow, since the closest air
station is in Traverse City, and a
Copper Country rescue would simply take
too long. With the help of a new
forty-seven foot life boat, local crews
can conduct search and rescue missions
much faster. Having a facility here to
respond is critical, as the ability to
survive in water this cold is short.
Rescue people need to get there
quickly.

U.S. Coast Guard personnel work to
ensure the waters stay safe, as an
increasing number of boats take to Lake
Superior and the Portage Lake shipping
canal. This station is responsible for
covering the area from Big Bay to Isle
Royale to Ontonagon and in bad weather,

from Marquette to Isle Royale to Bay-
field, Wisconsin. This Coast Guard
facility and the station in Saint
Ignace are the only two in the country
which perform search and rescue
missions along with law enforcement and
navigation.

In addition to maintaining
lighthouses, conducting search and
rescues, protecting marine environ-
ments, responding to pollution
incidents, enforces immigration and
custom laws, and cleaning and maintaining equipment, the Coast Guard is
responsible for marine law enforcement.
The U.S. Coast Guard is the premier law
enforcement on the water. The State
Police, County Sheriff Departments and
Department of Natural Resources don't
have the authority or jurisdiction or
the manpower the U.S. Coast Guard does.

Also, with fifteen lighthouses
from Ontonagon to Isle Royale to
Marquette, the crew stays busy with
maintenance work.

Citizens from the village of
Dollar Bay celebrated 100 years of its
history from June 27 through July 4,
1987.

The celebration, under the
chairmanship of L. Dennis Lahikainen,
began with the Copper Country Firemen's
Tournament; it kicked off on June 27th
with games and later a parade which
included antique cars, and a baseball
tournament. Beard judging and a

firemen's ball were included. Banners were hung over the main street as the town's birthday approached.

The next day, athletes participated in the Triathlon, an amateur log rolling contest, Clydesdale wagon rides, baseball and a community picnic. They also had lumberjack shows, a mini-museum, arts and crafts exhibits and the reunion. Music was available from Averice, the Weekend Cowboy Band, Frankie Yankovic, gospel concert, and many jam sessions.

Other events included martial arts demonstration, fireworks, sky divers, a statue dedication, placement of the time capsule, an all school reunion, and a chicken barbecue. The centennial committee also produced a book on the history of Dollar Bay. It was dedicated to the Reverend James L. Johnson, a native son of Dollar Bay, who died during the authorship of the centennial book.

"The Pioneer" a 350-pound life-size bronze statue, which took three months to make, was dedicated on Saturday July 4, 1987. Russell "Rusty" Hellman was the speaker for the dedication. The statue was a combined effort of two local artists, Dan Gawura of Calumet, who cast the statue, and Dennis Lahikainen of Dollar Bay, who sculpted the clay model. Lahikainen worked on the clay model for six months during his spare time.

The statue rests on a masonary

pedestal built by Dollar Bay residents. Cut granite field stones were placed around the base which hold a plaque. The time capsule was sealed in the statue by David Joyal and Patrick Foley.

This statue can be seen in a park on the corner of Main Street and Fir Avenue. This parcel of land was once the property of the Dollar Bay Land and Improvement Company. On the Fourth of July 1962, Osceola Township Supervisor Victor Johnson was presented with the deed for the new park.

In June of 1934 an ERA labor force constructed the park that was occupied by the Donlan House (hotel). The ERA employees transformed an "eyesore" into a grassy plot surrounded by maple trees. They erected a flag pole, placed benches around the park, and built a drinking fountain which was made of metal and placed on a concrete slab. Since the water was running all of the time, neighboring cows would stop and take a drink. The park was dedicated on Friday, June 23, 1934, by Hugo Lundman, chief speaker; Bert Neveau, refreshments; Bert Beaudette, caretaker and Carl Stoor, honorary band leader.

SOURCES

The references listed below were used in gathering information to aid in the writing of this publication. Not all of the sources are listed, however, as many people of the Copper Country provided much information.

I particularly used the resources of the Michigan Technological University Library and the Daily Mining Gazette, both of Houghton, Michigan. I am indebted to Verna K. Masters, Paulette G. Morin and Erik C. Nordberg of the Michigan Technological University for their assistance in the library archives.

PUBLICATIONS

Dollar Bay, Michigan, Centennial, 1887 - 1987, 100 Dollar Bay Etchings

St. Francis d'Assissi, Dollar Bay, Michigan, 1892 - 1967, Diamond Jubilee

75th Anniversary, 1900 - 1975, First Lutheran Church, Dollar Bay, Michigan, Pearl Stoor, Editor

History of the Upper Peninsula of Michigan, published by the Western Historical Company, 1883

A History of the Northern Peninsula of Michigan, by Alvah L. Sawyer, 1911

History of the Diocese of Sault Ste.
Marie and Marquette, by Rev. Antoine
Ivan Rezek, Vol. II, 1907

National Archives Microfilm
Publications, copy 841, roll number
60, Record of Appointment of
Postmasters, 1832 through September
30, 1971

Upper Michigan Postal History and
Postmarks, by William J. Taylor,
1988

The Copper Handbook, by Horace J.
Stevens, Vol's II, V and XI

U.S. Census Reports, Washington, D.C.

Condensed Historical Sketches for each
of Michigan's Counties, by Milo M.
Quaife, 1940

Boom Copper: The Story of the First
U.S. Mining Boom, by Angus Murdoch,
1964

Information of the Copper Country:
containing general information of
the Copper Country, Its Towns and
Villages, Mines and Mining Interests,
published by the Standard Publishing
Company, Houghton, Michigan, 1890

Some Copper Country Names and Places,
by Clarence J. Monette, 1975

Early Days of the Lake Superior Copper
Country, by Orrin W. Robinson, 1938

A True Description of the Lake Superior
Country; Its Rivers, Coasts, Bays,
Harbours, Islands, and Commerce,
by John R. St. John, 1846

Folk Traditions of the Upper Peninsula,
by Richard M. Dorson, Vol. 31 of the
Michigan History Magazine, March 1947

NEWSPAPERS

The Portage Lake Mining Gazette,
Houghton, Michigan

The Daily Mining Gazette, Houghton,
Michigan

The Evening Journal, Calumet, Michigan

The Keweenaw Miner, Mohawk, Michigan

The Torch Lake Times, Lake Linden,
Michigan

The Native Copper Times, Lake Linden,
Michigan

Lake Superior News and Journal,
Marquette, Michigan

Lake Superior Miner, Marquette,
Michigan

OTHER SOURCES

Memories, Technical information and
proof reading of this publication
pertaining to Dollar Bay's local
history by resident Waldo Backman,
village local historian, Dollar Bay,
Michigan

A History of the Osceola Township
Office Building, by John Backman,
Dollar Bay, Michigan.

John also provided detailed
assistance as well as written and
printed materials pertaining to
the local history of Dollar Bay.
Like his Father Waldo, he assisted in
the proof reading of this material.

Written material from Kenneth L.
Anderson, of Dollar Bay, Michigan

Postal data from William C. Allen
of Escanaba, Michigan

Assistance from the Library Archives,
Michigan Technological University,
Houghton, Michigan

Assistance from the Library Archives,
Suomi College, Hancock, Michigan

Keweenaw Historical Society Collection,
maintained at the Michigan
Technological University Library,
Archives Section, Houghton, Michigan

Roy Drier Collection, maintained at
the Michigan Technological University
Library, Archives Section, Houghton,
Michigan

ADD THIS COPPER COUNTRY LOCAL HISTORY
SERIES TO YOUR PERSONAL LIBRARY

COR-AGO, A LAKE LINDEN MEDICINE COMPANY
First of a local history series

A COPPER COUNTRY LOGGER'S TALE
Second of a local history series

GREGORYVILLE - THE HISTORY OF A HAMLET LOCATED ACROSS
FROM LAKE LINDEN, MICHIGAN
Third of a local history series

WHITE CITY - THE HISTORY OF AN EARLY COPPER COUNTRY
RECREATION AREA
Fourth of a local history series

SOME COPPER COUNTRY NAMES AND PLACES
Fifth of a local history series

THE HISTORY OF LAKE LINDEN, MICHIGAN
Sixth of a local history series

THE HISTORY OF JACOBSVILLE AND ITS SANDSTONE QUARRIES
Seventh of a local history series

THE HISTORY OF COPPER HARBOR, MICHIGAN
Eight of a local history series

THE HISTORY OF EAGLE HARBOR, MICHIGAN
Ninth of a local history series

LAKE LINDEN'S YESTERDAY - A PICTORIAL HISTORY, VOLUME I
Tenth of a local history series

THE HISTORY OF EAGLE RIVER, MICHIGAN
Eleventh of a local history series

JOSEPH BOSCH AND THE BOSCH BREWING COMPANY
Twelfth of a local history series

COPPER FALLS - JUST A MEMORY
  Thirteenth of a local history series

THE CALUMET THEATRE
  Fourteenth of a local history series

EARLY DAYS IN MOHAWK, MICHIGAN
  Fifteenth of a local history series

LAKE LINDEN'S YESTERDAY - A PICTORIAL HISTORY, VOLUME II
  Sixteenth of a local history series

THE KEWEENAW WATERWAY
  Seventeenth of a local history series

A BRIEF HISTORY OF AHMEEK, MICHIGAN
  Eighteenth of a local history series

ALL ABOUT MANDAN, MICHIGAN
  Nineteenth of a local history series

HANCOCK, MICHIGAN, REMEMBERED, VOLUME I
  Twentieth of a local history series

THE SETTLING OF COPPER CITY, MICHIGAN
  Twenty-first of a local history series

LAKE LINDEN'S YESTERDAY - A PICTORIAL HISTORY, VOLUME III
  Twenty-second of a local history series

PAINESDALE, MICHIGAN - OLD AND NEW
  Twenty-third of a local history series

SOME OF THE BEST FROM C & H NEWS - VIEWS, VOLUME I
  Twenty-fourth of a local history series

HANCOCK, MICHIGAN, REMEMBERED - CHURCHES OF HANCOCK,
VOLUME II
  Twenty-fifth of a local history series

OJIBWAY, MICHIGAN, A FORGOTTEN VILLAGE
  Twenty-sixth of a local history series

LAURIUM, MICHIGAN'S EARLY DAYS
  Twenty-seventh of a local history series

DELAWARE, MICHIGAN, ITS HISTORY
  Twenty-eight of a local history series

LAKE LINDEN'S LIVING HISTORY - 1985
  Twenty-ninth of a local history series

SOME OF THE BEST FROM C & H NEWS - VIEWS, VOLUME II
  Thirtieth of a local history series

THE GAY, MICHIGAN, STORY
  Thirty-first of a local history series

EARLY RED JACKET AND CALUMET IN PICTURES, VOLUME I
  Thirty-second of a local history series

LAKE LINDEN'S DISASTROUS FIRE OF 1887
  Thirty-third of a local history series

PHOENIX, MICHIGAN'S HISTORY
  Thirty-fourth of a local history series

FREDA, MICHIGAN, END OF THE ROAD
  Thirty-fifth of a local history series

HOUGHTON IN PICTURES
  Thirty-sixth of a local history series

THE COPPER RANGE RAILROAD
  Thirty-seventh of a local history series

LAC LA BELLE
  Thirty-eight of a local history series

TRIMOUNTAIN AND ITS COPPER MINES
  Thirty-ninth of a local history series

EARLY RED JACKET AND CALUMET IN PICTURES, VOLUME II
  Fortieth of a local history series

UPPER PENINSULA'S WOLVERINE
   Forty-first of a local history series

REDRIDGE AND ITS STEEL DAM
   Forty-second of a local history series

THE MINERAL RANGE RAILROAD
   Forty-third of a local history series

WINONA AND THE KING PHILIP PROPERTIES
   Forty-fourth of a local history series

ATLANTIC MINE: PHOTOGRAPHS FROM THE
HAROLD H. HEIKKINEN COLLECTION
   Forty-fifth of a local history series

SOME OF THE BEST FROM C & H NEWS - VIEWS, VOLUME III
   Forty-sixth of a local history series

ALLOUEZ, NEW ALLOUEZ AND BUMBLETOWN
   Forty-seventh of a local history series

SOME FATAL ACCIDENTS IN THE ATLANTIC, BALTIC,
CHAMPION, TRIMOUNTAIN AND WINONA COPPER MINES
   Forty-eighth of a local history series

EARLY SOUTH RANGE, MICHIGAN, VOLUME I
   Forty-ninth of a local history series

CENTRAL MINE: A GHOST TOWN
   Fiftieth of a local history series

BALTIC, MICHIGAN
   Fifty-first of a local history series

KEWEENAW CENTRAL RAILROAD AND THE CRESTVIEW RESORT
   Fifty-second of a local history series

CLIFTON AND THE CLIFF MINE
   Fifty-third of a local history series

DOLLAR BAY, MICHIGAN
   Fifty-fourth of a local history series